Mometrix TEST PREPARATION

Regents

Success Strategies Geometry

Dear Future Exam Success Story

First of all, **THANK YOU** for purchasing Mometrix study materials!

Second, congratulations! You are one of the few determined test-takers who are committed to doing whatever it takes to excel on your exam. **You have come to the right place.** We developed these study materials with one goal in mind: to deliver you the information you need in a format that's concise and easy to use.

In addition to optimizing your guide for the content of the test, we've outlined our recommended steps for breaking down the preparation process into small, attainable goals so you can make sure you stay on track.

We've also analyzed the entire test-taking process, identifying the most common pitfalls and showing how you can overcome them and be ready for any curveball the test throws you.

Standardized testing is one of the biggest obstacles on your road to success, which only increases the importance of doing well in the high-pressure, high-stakes environment of test day. Your results on this test could have a significant impact on your future, and this guide provides the information and practical advice to help you achieve your full potential on test day.

Your success is our success

We would love to hear from you! If you would like to share the story of your exam success or if you have any questions or comments in regard to our products, please contact us at **800-673-8175** or **support@mometrix.com**.

Thanks again for your business and we wish you continued success!

Sincerely,
The Mometrix Test Preparation Team

Table of Contents

Introduction 1

Strategy #1 – Plan Big, Study Small 2

Strategy #2 – Make Your Studying Count 3

Strategy #3 – Practice the Right Way 4

Strategy #4 – Pace Yourself 6

Test-Taking Strategies 7

Geometry 11

- Parabolas 11
- Trigonometric Functions 11
- Points, Lines, and Planes 14
- Angles 16
- Polygons 18
- Apothem and Radius 19
- Congruence and Similarity 20
- Line of Symmetry 21
- Triangles 22
- Triangle Properties 23
- Quadrilaterals 25
- Circles 30
- Circle Properties 31
- Transformations 33
- 3D Shapes 35
- Pythagorean Theorem 39
- Trigonometric Formulas 39
- Ellipses and Hyperbolas 40
- Conic Sections 40
- Chapter Quiz 41

Regents Practice Test #1 42

Answer Key and Explanations for Test #1 56

Regents Practice Test #2 66

Answer Key and Explanations for Test #2 79

How to Overcome Test Anxiety 88

Online Resources 94

Introduction

Thank you for purchasing this resource! You have made the choice to prepare yourself for a test that could have a huge impact on your future, and this guide is designed to help you be fully ready for test day. Obviously, it's important to have a solid understanding of the test material, but you also need to be prepared for the unique environment and stressors of the test, so that you can perform to the best of your abilities.

For this purpose, the first section that appears in this guide is the **Success Strategies**. We've devoted countless hours to meticulously researching what works and what doesn't, and we've boiled down our findings to the five most impactful steps you can take to improve your performance on the test. We start at the beginning with study planning and move through the preparation process, all the way to the testing strategies that will help you get the most out of what you know when you're finally sitting in front of the test.

We recommend that you start preparing for your test as far in advance as possible. However, if you've bought this guide as a last-minute study resource and only have a few days before your test, we recommend that you skip over the first two Success Strategies since they address a long-term study plan.

If you struggle with **test anxiety**, we strongly encourage you to check out our recommendations for how you can overcome it. Test anxiety is a formidable foe, but it can be beaten, and we want to make sure you have the tools you need to defeat it.

Strategy #1 – Plan Big, Study Small

There's a lot riding on your performance. If you want to ace this test, you're going to need to keep your skills sharp and the material fresh in your mind. You need a plan that lets you review everything you need to know while still fitting in your schedule. We'll break this strategy down into three categories.

Information Organization

Start with the information you already have: the official test outline. From this, you can make a complete list of all the concepts you need to cover before the test. Organize these concepts into groups that can be studied together, and create a list of any related vocabulary you need to learn so you can brush up on any difficult terms. You'll want to keep this vocabulary list handy once you actually start studying since you may need to add to it along the way.

Time Management

Once you have your set of study concepts, decide how to spread them out over the time you have left before the test. Break your study plan into small, clear goals so you have a manageable task for each day and know exactly what you're doing. Then just focus on one small step at a time. When you manage your time this way, you don't need to spend hours at a time studying. Studying a small block of content for a short period each day helps you retain information better and avoid stressing over how much you have left to do. You can relax knowing that you have a plan to cover everything in time. In order for this strategy to be effective though, you have to start studying early and stick to your schedule. Avoid the exhaustion and futility that comes from last-minute cramming!

Study Environment

The environment you study in has a big impact on your learning. Studying in a coffee shop, while probably more enjoyable, is not likely to be as fruitful as studying in a quiet room. It's important to keep distractions to a minimum. You're only planning to study for a short block of time, so make the most of it. Don't pause to check your phone or get up to find a snack. It's also important to **avoid multitasking**. Research has consistently shown that multitasking will make your studying dramatically less effective. Your study area should also be comfortable and well-lit so you don't have the distraction of straining your eyes or sitting on an uncomfortable chair.

The time of day you study is also important. You want to be rested and alert. Don't wait until just before bedtime. Study when you'll be most likely to comprehend and remember. Even better, if you know what time of day your test will be, set that time aside for study. That way your brain will be used to working on that subject at that specific time and you'll have a better chance of recalling information.

Finally, it can be helpful to team up with others who are studying for the same test. Your actual studying should be done in as isolated an environment as possible, but the work of organizing the information and setting up the study plan can be divided up. In between study sessions, you can discuss with your teammates the concepts that you're all studying and quiz each other on the details. Just be sure that your teammates are as serious about the test as you are. If you find that your study time is being replaced with social time, you might need to find a new team.

Strategy #2 – Make Your Studying Count

You're devoting a lot of time and effort to preparing for this test, so you want to be absolutely certain it will pay off. This means doing more than just reading the content and hoping you can remember it on test day. It's important to make every minute of study count. There are two main areas you can focus on to make your studying count.

Retention

It doesn't matter how much time you study if you can't remember the material. You need to make sure you are retaining the concepts. To check your retention of the information you're learning, try recalling it at later times with minimal prompting. Try carrying around flashcards and glance at one or two from time to time or ask a friend who's also studying for the test to quiz you.

To enhance your retention, look for ways to put the information into practice so that you can apply it rather than simply recalling it. If you're using the information in practical ways, it will be much easier to remember. Similarly, it helps to solidify a concept in your mind if you're not only reading it to yourself but also explaining it to someone else. Ask a friend to let you teach them about a concept you're a little shaky on (or speak aloud to an imaginary audience if necessary). As you try to summarize, define, give examples, and answer your friend's questions, you'll understand the concepts better and they will stay with you longer. Finally, step back for a big picture view and ask yourself how each piece of information fits with the whole subject. When you link the different concepts together and see them working together as a whole, it's easier to remember the individual components.

Finally, practice showing your work on any multi-step problems, even if you're just studying. Writing out each step you take to solve a problem will help solidify the process in your mind, and you'll be more likely to remember it during the test.

Modality

Modality simply refers to the means or method by which you study. Choosing a study modality that fits your own individual learning style is crucial. No two people learn best in exactly the same way, so it's important to know your strengths and use them to your advantage.

For example, if you learn best by visualization, focus on visualizing a concept in your mind and draw an image or a diagram. Try color-coding your notes, illustrating them, or creating symbols that will trigger your mind to recall a learned concept. If you learn best by hearing or discussing information, find a study partner who learns the same way or read aloud to yourself. Think about how to put the information in your own words. Imagine that you are giving a lecture on the topic and record yourself so you can listen to it later.

For any learning style, flashcards can be helpful. Organize the information so you can take advantage of spare moments to review. Underline key words or phrases. Use different colors for different categories. Mnemonic devices (such as creating a short list in which every item starts with the same letter) can also help with retention. Find what works best for you and use it to store the information in your mind most effectively and easily.

Strategy #3 – Practice the Right Way

Your success on test day depends not only on how many hours you put into preparing, but also on whether you prepared the right way. It's good to check along the way to see if your studying is paying off. One of the most effective ways to do this is by taking practice tests to evaluate your progress. Practice tests are useful because they show exactly where you need to improve. Every time you take a practice test, pay special attention to these three groups of questions:

- The questions you got wrong
- The questions you had to guess on, even if you guessed right
- The questions you found difficult or slow to work through

This will show you exactly what your weak areas are, and where you need to devote more study time. Ask yourself why each of these questions gave you trouble. Was it because you didn't understand the material? Was it because you didn't remember the vocabulary? Do you need more repetitions on this type of question to build speed and confidence? Dig into those questions and figure out how you can strengthen your weak areas as you go back to review the material.

Additionally, many practice tests have a section explaining the answer choices. It can be tempting to read the explanation and think that you now have a good understanding of the concept. However, an explanation likely only covers part of the question's broader context. Even if the explanation makes perfect sense, **go back and investigate** every concept related to the question until you're positive you have a thorough understanding.

As you go along, keep in mind that the practice test is just that: practice. Memorizing these questions and answers will not be very helpful on the actual test because it is unlikely to have any of the same exact questions. If you only know the right answers to the sample questions, you won't be prepared for the real thing. **Study the concepts** until you understand them fully, and then you'll be able to answer any question that shows up on the test.

It's important to wait on the practice tests until you're ready. If you take a test on your first day of study, you may be overwhelmed by the amount of material covered and how much you need to learn. Work up to it gradually.

On test day, you'll need to be prepared for answering questions, managing your time, and using the test-taking strategies you've learned. It's a lot to balance, like a mental marathon that will have a big impact on your future. Like training for a marathon, you'll need to start slowly and work your way up. When test day arrives, you'll be ready.

Start with the strategies you've read in the first two Success Strategies—plan your course and study in the way that works best for you. If you have time, consider using multiple study resources to get different approaches to the same concepts. It can be helpful to see difficult concepts from more than one angle. Then find a good source for practice tests. Many times, the test website will suggest potential study resources or provide sample tests.

Practice Test Strategy

If you're able to find at least three practice tests, we recommend this strategy:

Untimed and Open-Book Practice

Take the first test with no time constraints and with your notes and study guide handy. Take your time and focus on applying the strategies you've learned.

Timed and Open-Book Practice

Take the second practice test open-book as well, but set a timer and practice pacing yourself to finish in time.

Timed and Closed-Book Practice

Take any other practice tests as if it were test day. Set a timer and put away your study materials. Sit at a table or desk in a quiet room, imagine yourself at the testing center, and answer questions as quickly and accurately as possible.

Keep repeating timed and closed-book tests on a regular basis until you run out of practice tests or it's time for the actual test. Your mind will be ready for the schedule and stress of test day, and you'll be able to focus on recalling the material you've learned.

Strategy #4 – Pace Yourself

Once you're fully prepared for the material on the test, your biggest challenge on test day will be managing your time. Just knowing that the clock is ticking can make you panic even if you have plenty of time left. Work on pacing yourself so you can build confidence against the time constraints of the exam. Pacing is a difficult skill to master, especially in a high-pressure environment, so **practice is vital**.

Set time expectations for your pace based on how much time is available. For example, if a section has 60 questions and the time limit is 30 minutes, you know you have to average 30 seconds or less per question in order to answer them all. Although 30 seconds is the hard limit, set 25 seconds per question as your goal, so you reserve extra time to spend on harder questions. When you budget extra time for the harder questions, you no longer have any reason to stress when those questions take longer to answer.

Don't let this time expectation distract you from working through the test at a calm, steady pace, but keep it in mind so you don't spend too much time on any one question. Recognize that taking extra time on one question you don't understand may keep you from answering two that you do understand later in the test. If your time limit for a question is up and you're still not sure of the answer, mark it and move on, and come back to it later if the time and the test format allow. If the testing format doesn't allow you to return to earlier questions, just make an educated guess; then put it out of your mind and move on.

On the easier questions, be careful not to rush. It may seem wise to hurry through them so you have more time for the challenging ones, but it's not worth missing one if you know the concept and just didn't take the time to read the question fully. Work efficiently but make sure you understand the question and have looked at all of the answer choices, since more than one may seem right at first.

Even if you're paying attention to the time, you may find yourself a little behind at some point. You should speed up to get back on track, but do so wisely. Don't panic; just take a few seconds less on each question until you're caught up. Don't guess without thinking, but do look through the answer choices and eliminate any you know are wrong. If you can get down to two choices, it is often worthwhile to guess from those. Once you've chosen an answer, move on and don't dwell on any that you skipped or had to hurry through. If a question was taking too long, chances are it was one of the harder ones, so you weren't as likely to get it right anyway.

On the other hand, if you find yourself getting ahead of schedule, it may be beneficial to slow down a little. The more quickly you work, the more likely you are to make a careless mistake that will affect your score. You've budgeted time for each question, so don't be afraid to spend that time. Practice an efficient but careful pace to get the most out of the time you have.

Test-Taking Strategies

This section contains a list of test-taking strategies that you may find helpful as you work through the test. By taking what you know and applying logical thought, you can maximize your chances of answering any question correctly!

It is very important to realize that every question is different and every person is different: no single strategy will work on every question, and no single strategy will work for every person. That's why we've included all of them here, so you can try them out and determine which ones work best for different types of questions and which ones work best for you.

Question Strategies

✓ Read Carefully

Read the question and the answer choices carefully. Don't miss the question because you misread the terms. You have plenty of time to read each question thoroughly and make sure you understand what is being asked. Yet a happy medium must be attained, so don't waste too much time. You must read carefully and efficiently.

✓ Contextual Clues

Look for contextual clues. If the question includes a word you are not familiar with, look at the immediate context for some indication of what the word might mean. Contextual clues can often give you all the information you need to decipher the meaning of an unfamiliar word. Even if you can't determine the meaning, you may be able to narrow down the possibilities enough to make a solid guess at the answer to the question.

✓ Prefixes

If you're having trouble with a word in the question or answer choices, try dissecting it. Take advantage of every clue that the word might include. Prefixes can be a huge help. Usually, they allow you to determine a basic meaning. *Pre-* means before, *post-* means after, *pro-* is positive, *de-* is negative. From prefixes, you can get an idea of the general meaning of the word and try to put it into context.

✓ Hedge Words

Watch out for critical hedge words, such as *likely, may, can, often, almost, mostly, usually, generally, rarely,* and *sometimes.* Question writers insert these hedge phrases to cover every possibility. Often an answer choice will be wrong simply because it leaves no room for exception. Be on guard for answer choices that have definitive words such as *exactly* and *always.*

✓ Switchback Words

Stay alert for *switchbacks.* These are the words and phrases frequently used to alert you to shifts in thought. The most common switchback words are *but, although,* and *however.* Others include *nevertheless, on the other hand, even though, while, in spite of, despite,* and *regardless of.* Switchback words are important to catch because they can change the direction of the question or an answer choice.

✓ FACE VALUE

When in doubt, use common sense. Accept the situation in the problem at face value. Don't read too much into it. These problems will not require you to make wild assumptions. If you have to go beyond creativity and warp time or space in order to have an answer choice fit the question, then you should move on and consider the other answer choices. These are normal problems rooted in reality. The applicable relationship or explanation may not be readily apparent, but it is there for you to figure out. Use your common sense to interpret anything that isn't clear.

Answer Choice Strategies

✓ ANSWER SELECTION

The most thorough way to pick an answer choice is to identify and eliminate wrong answers until only one is left, then confirm it is the correct answer. Sometimes an answer choice may immediately seem right, but be careful. The test writers will usually put more than one reasonable answer choice on each question, so take a second to read all of them and make sure that the other choices are not equally obvious. As long as you have time left, it is better to read every answer choice than to pick the first one that looks right without checking the others.

✓ ANSWER CHOICE FAMILIES

An answer choice family consists of two (in rare cases, three) answer choices that are very similar in construction and cannot all be true at the same time. If you see two answer choices that are direct opposites or parallels, one of them is usually the correct answer. For instance, if one answer choice says that quantity *x* increases and another either says that quantity *x* decreases (opposite) or says that quantity *y* increases (parallel), then those answer choices would fall into the same family. An answer choice that doesn't match the construction of the answer choice family is more likely to be incorrect. Most questions will not have answer choice families, but when they do appear, you should be prepared to recognize them.

✓ ELIMINATE ANSWERS

Eliminate answer choices as soon as you realize they are wrong, but make sure you consider all possibilities. If you are eliminating answer choices and realize that the last one you are left with is also wrong, don't panic. Start over and consider each choice again. There may be something you missed the first time that you will realize on the second pass.

✓ AVOID FACT TRAPS

Don't be distracted by an answer choice that is factually true but doesn't answer the question. You are looking for the choice that answers the question. Stay focused on what the question is asking for so you don't accidentally pick an answer that is true but incorrect. Always go back to the question and make sure the answer choice you've selected actually answers the question and is not merely a true statement.

✓ EXTREME STATEMENTS

In general, you should avoid answers that put forth extreme actions as standard practice or proclaim controversial ideas as established fact. An answer choice that states the "process should be used in certain situations, if..." is much more likely to be correct than one that states the "process should be discontinued completely." The first is a calm rational statement and doesn't even make a definitive, uncompromising stance, using a hedge word *if* to provide wiggle room, whereas the second choice is far more extreme.

✅ BENCHMARK

As you read through the answer choices and you come across one that seems to answer the question well, mentally select that answer choice. This is not your final answer, but it's the one that will help you evaluate the other answer choices. The one that you selected is your benchmark or standard for judging each of the other answer choices. Every other answer choice must be compared to your benchmark. That choice is correct until proven otherwise by another answer choice beating it. If you find a better answer, then that one becomes your new benchmark. Once you've decided that no other choice answers the question as well as your benchmark, you have your final answer.

✅ PREDICT THE ANSWER

Before you even start looking at the answer choices, it is often best to try to predict the answer. When you come up with the answer on your own, it is easier to avoid distractions and traps because you will know exactly what to look for. The right answer choice is unlikely to be word-for-word what you came up with, but it should be a close match. Even if you are confident that you have the right answer, you should still take the time to read each option before moving on.

General Strategies

✅ TOUGH QUESTIONS

If you are stumped on a problem or it appears too hard or too difficult, don't waste time. Move on! Remember though, if you can quickly check for obviously incorrect answer choices, your chances of guessing correctly are greatly improved. Before you completely give up, at least try to knock out a couple of possible answers. Eliminate what you can and then guess at the remaining answer choices before moving on.

✅ CHECK YOUR WORK

Since you will probably not know every term listed and the answer to every question, it is important that you get credit for the ones that you do know. Don't miss any questions through careless mistakes. If at all possible, try to take a second to look back over your answer selection and make sure you've selected the correct answer choice and haven't made a costly careless mistake (such as marking an answer choice that you didn't mean to mark). This quick double check should more than pay for itself in caught mistakes for the time it costs.

✅ PACE YOURSELF

It's easy to be overwhelmed when you're looking at a page full of questions; your mind is confused and full of random thoughts, and the clock is ticking down faster than you would like. Calm down and maintain the pace that you have set for yourself. Especially as you get down to the last few minutes of the test, don't let the small numbers on the clock make you panic. As long as you are on track by monitoring your pace, you are guaranteed to have time for each question.

✅ DON'T RUSH

It is very easy to make errors when you are in a hurry. Maintaining a fast pace in answering questions is pointless if it makes you miss questions that you would have gotten right otherwise. Test writers like to include distracting information and wrong answers that seem right. Taking a little extra time to avoid careless mistakes can make all the difference in your test score. Find a pace that allows you to be confident in the answers that you select.

⊘ KEEP MOVING

Panicking will not help you pass the test, so do your best to stay calm and keep moving. Taking deep breaths and going through the answer elimination steps you practiced can help to break through a stress barrier and keep your pace.

Final Notes

The combination of a solid foundation of content knowledge and the confidence that comes from practicing your plan for applying that knowledge is the key to maximizing your performance on test day. As your foundation of content knowledge is built up and strengthened, you'll find that the strategies included in this chapter become more and more effective in helping you quickly sift through the distractions and traps of the test to isolate the correct answer.

Now that you're preparing to move forward into the test content chapters of this book, be sure to keep your goal in mind. As you read, think about how you will be able to apply this information on the test. If you've already seen sample questions for the test and you have an idea of the question format and style, try to come up with questions of your own that you can answer based on what you're reading. This will give you valuable practice applying your knowledge in the same ways you can expect to on test day.

Good luck and good studying!

Geometry

Parabolas

A **parabola** is the set of all points in a plane that are equidistant from a fixed line, called the **directrix**, and a fixed point not on the line, called the **focus**. The **axis** is the line perpendicular to the directrix that passes through the focus.

For parabolas that open up or down, the standard equation is $(x - h)^2 = 4c(y - k)$, where h, c, and k are coefficients. If c is positive, the parabola opens up. If c is negative, the parabola opens down. The vertex is the point (h, k). The directrix is the line having the equation $y = -c + k$, and the focus is the point $(h, c + k)$.

For parabolas that open left or right, the standard equation is $(y - k)^2 = 4c(x - h)$, where k, c, and h are coefficients. If c is positive, the parabola opens to the right. If c is negative, the parabola opens to the left. The vertex is the point (h, k). The directrix is the line having the equation $x = -c + h$, and the focus is the point $(c + h, k)$.

Review Video: Parabolas
Visit mometrix.com/academy and enter code: 129187

Review Video: Vertex of a Parabola
Visit mometrix.com/academy and enter code: 272300

Review Video: How to Convert Between Standard Form and Vertex Form
Visit mometrix.com/academy and enter code: 916601

Trigonometric Functions

The basic trigonometric functions are sine (abbreviated 'sin'), cosine (abbreviated 'cos'), and tangent (abbreviated 'tan'). The simplest way to think of them is as describing the ratio of the side lengths of a right triangle in relation to the angles of the triangle.

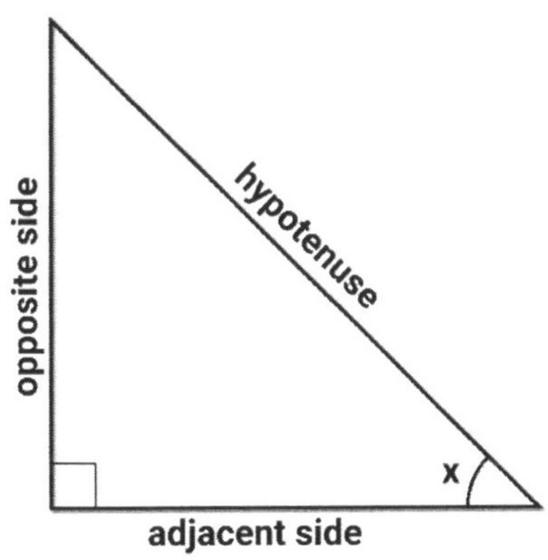

$$\sin x = \frac{\text{opposite side}}{\text{hypotenuse}}$$
$$\cos x = \frac{\text{adjacent side}}{\text{hypotenuse}}$$
$$\tan x = \frac{\text{opposite side}}{\text{adjacent side}}$$

Applying Trigonometric Functions

Suppose we have a point (x, y) at distance r from the origin such that the line segment between this point and the origin forms an angle of measure θ with the positive x-axis (We allow θ to be any real number, with the angle measured counterclockwise from the x-axis if $\theta > 0$ and clockwise if $\theta < 0$).

Then we can define the trigonometric functions sine, cosine, and tangent by the formulas $\sin\theta = y/r$, $\cos\theta = x/r$, and $\tan\theta = y/x$ (and their reciprocal functions cosecant, secant, and cotangent accordingly). These functions are periodic because increasing the angle θ by 2π radians (that is, $360°$) turns the line segment all the way around the origin so that it ends at the same point (x, y) again.

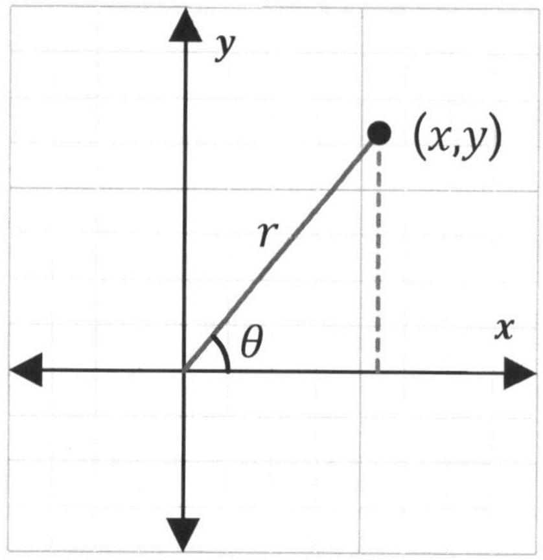

If the angle in the above diagram is acute, we can think of the line segment as the hypotenuse of a right triangle so that we get the familiar formulas $\sin\theta = (\text{opposite leg})/\text{hypotenuse}$, $\cos\theta = (\text{adjacent leg})/\text{hypotenuse}$, and $\tan\theta = (\text{opposite leg})/(\text{adjacent leg})$. In this form, the trigonometric functions are useful for finding missing sides of triangles. For example, suppose that standing 30 feet from the base of a tree, we have to look up at a $58°$ angle to see the top of the tree (see diagram). If we let x be the height of the tree, then we get the equation $\tan 58° = x/(30\text{ feet})$. Multiplying both sides of the equation by 30 gives us the height of the tree, namely, $x = 30\tan 58° \approx 48$ feet.

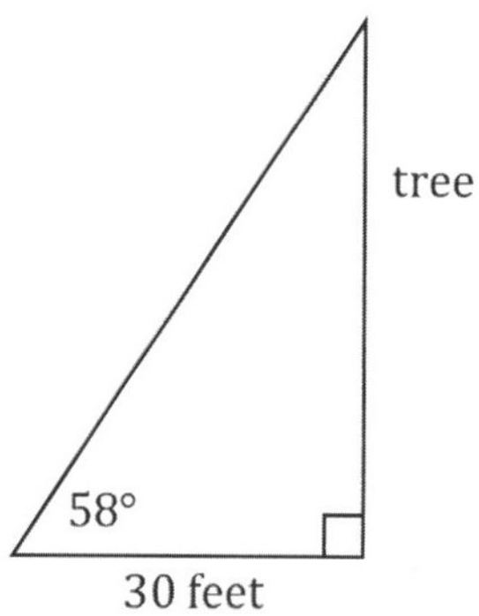

Graphing Trigonometric Functions

Sine

To graph the sine function, we let x (rather than θ) be the angle measure (usually in radians) and y be the value of the sine. That is, we graph the equation $y = \sin x$. From the definition of sine above we can show that $\sin 0 = 0$, $\sin(\pi/2) = 1$, $\sin\pi = 0$, $\sin(3\pi/2) = -1$, and $\sin 2\pi = 0$. Thus, the graph of the sine function begins at the origin, peaks at the point $(\pi/2, 1)$, crosses the x-axis at $(\pi, 0)$, has its lowest point at $(3\pi/2, -1)$, and returns to the x-axis at $(2\pi, 0)$. Because the sine function is periodic with period 2π radians (or $360°$), this curve represents one complete cycle of the graph. The remainder of the graph of $y = \sin x$ consists of infinitely many repetitions of this cycle, producing the familiar "sine wave."

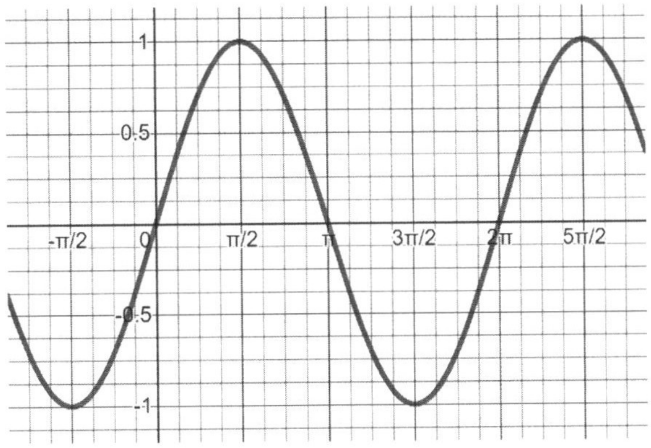

Review Video: Sine
Visit mometrix.com/academy and enter code: 193339

By suitable choice of the parameters A, B, C, and D, we can construct a "custom" sine function $y = A\sin(Bx + C) + D$ with any desired amplitude (the vertical distance the curve extends above and below its midline), period (distance between successive peaks), phase shift (horizontal shift), and midline (the horizontal line halfway between the peaks and troughs).

Cosine

Similarly, the graph of the cosine function is the graph of the equation $y = \cos x$. Proceeding as above, we get a graph with the same shape as that of the sine function but shifted by $\pi/2$ to the left.

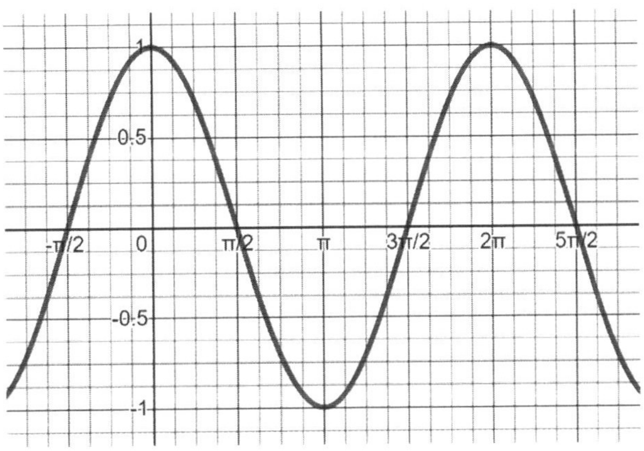

Review Video: Cosine
Visit mometrix.com/academy and enter code: 361120

As for the sine function, we can construct custom cosine graphs with desired amplitude, period, phase shift, and midline by choosing suitable values of the parameters in the equation $y = A\cos(Bx + C) + D$.

TANGENT

The graph of the tangent function (that is, the graph of the equation $y = \tan x$) turns out to be periodic with period π radians (or 180°). It consists of an infinite sequence of smooth curves crossing the x-axis at every multiple of π radians (180°) and having as asymptotes the vertical lines $x = \frac{k\pi}{2}$ radians ($x = k \times 90°$), for every odd integer k (which also means that the domain of the tangent function excludes these x-values).

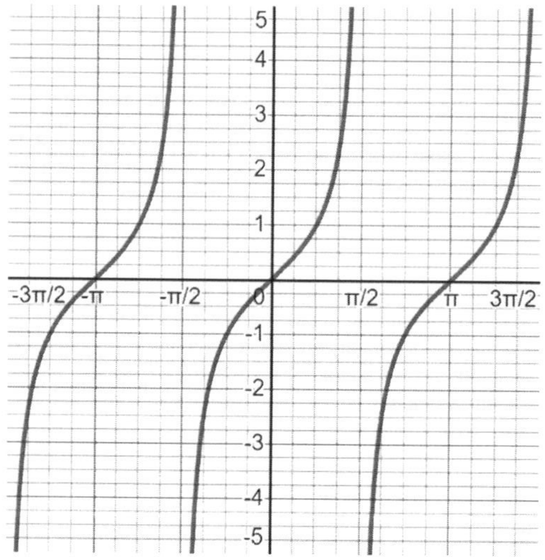

Review Video: Tangent
Visit mometrix.com/academy and enter code: 947639

Points, Lines, and Planes

POINTS AND LINES

A **point** is a fixed location in space, has no size or dimensions, and is commonly represented by a dot. A **line** is a set of points that extends infinitely in two opposite directions. It has length, but no width or depth. A line can be defined by any two distinct points that it contains. A **line segment** is a portion of a line that has definite endpoints. A **ray** is a portion of a line that extends from a single point on that line in one direction along the line. It has a definite beginning, but no ending.

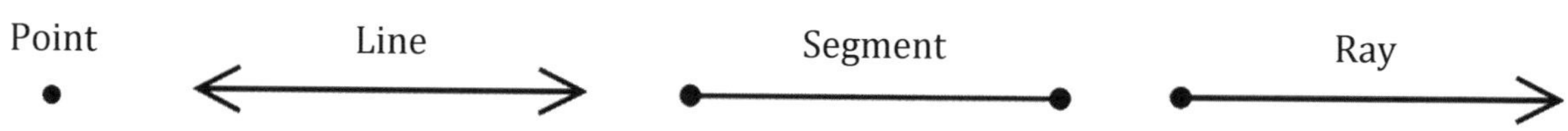

Points are **collinear** if there is a single line that passes through all of them. Otherwise, they are noncollinear. Two points are always collinear since two points define a line. Three points may be noncollinear. For example, the three vertices of a triangle are noncollinear since there is no line that goes through all three of them.

INTERACTIONS BETWEEN LINES

Intersecting lines are lines that have exactly one point in common. **Concurrent lines** are multiple lines that intersect at a single point. **Perpendicular lines** are lines that intersect at right angles. They are represented by the symbol ⊥. The shortest distance from a line to a point not on the line is a perpendicular segment from the point to the line. **Parallel lines** are lines in the same plane that have no points in common and never meet. Two distinct lines in a given plane are always either intersecting or parallel. **Skew lines** are two distinct lines in a three dimensional space that do not intersect and may also not be parallel because there is no single plane that contains them both.

Intersecting

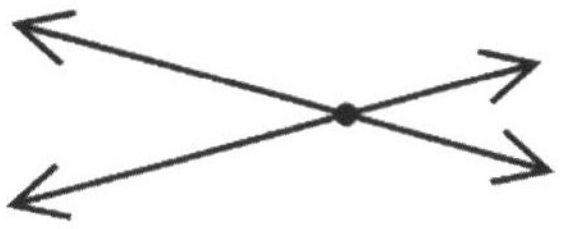

Concurrent

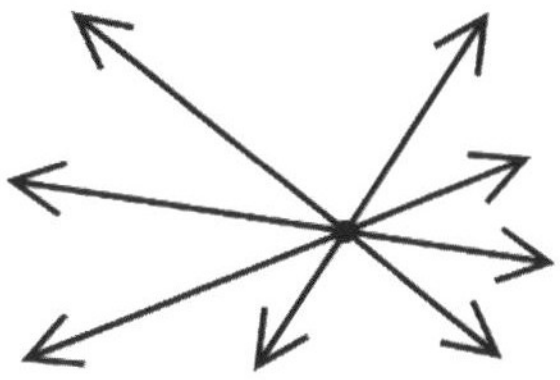

Perpendicular

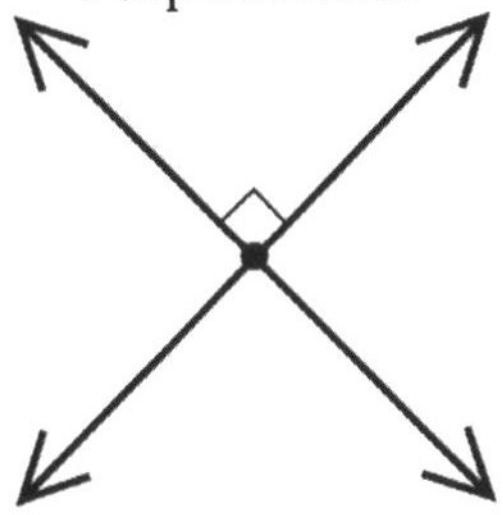

Parallel

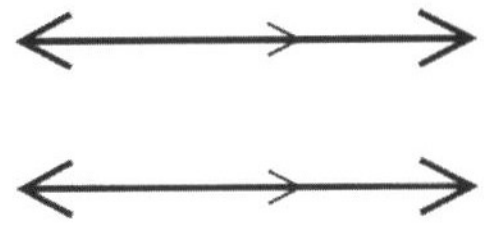

Review Video: Parallel and Perpendicular Lines
Visit mometrix.com/academy and enter code: 815923

A **transversal** is a line that intersects at least two other lines, which may or may not be parallel to one another. A transversal that intersects parallel lines is a common occurrence in geometry. A **bisector** is a line or line segment that divides another line segment into two equal lengths. A **perpendicular bisector** of a line segment is composed of points that are equidistant from the endpoints of the segment it is dividing.

Transversal

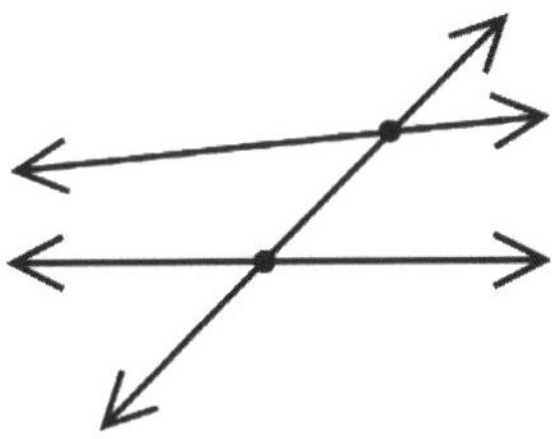

Bisector

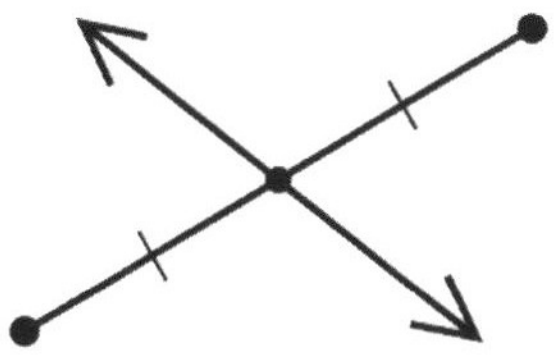

Perpendicular bisector

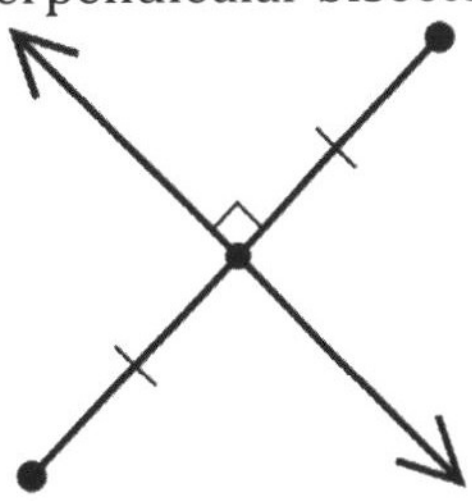

The **projection of a point on a line** is the point at which a perpendicular line drawn from the given point to the given line intersects the line. This is also the shortest distance from the given point to the line. The **projection of a segment on a line** is a segment whose endpoints are the points formed when perpendicular lines are drawn from the endpoints of the given segment to the given line. This is similar to the length a diagonal line appears to be when viewed from above.

Projection of a point on a line

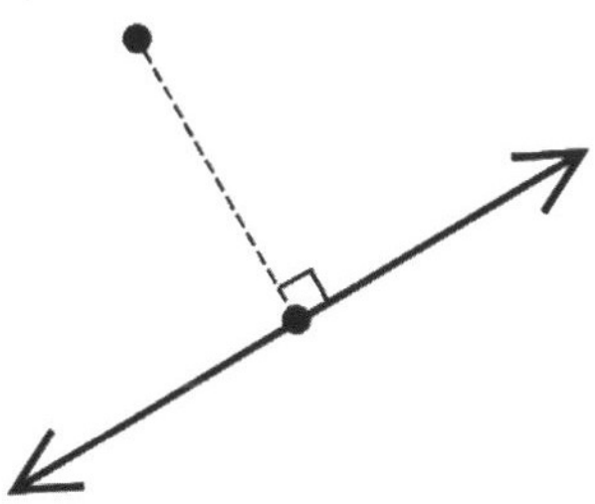

Projection of a segment on a line

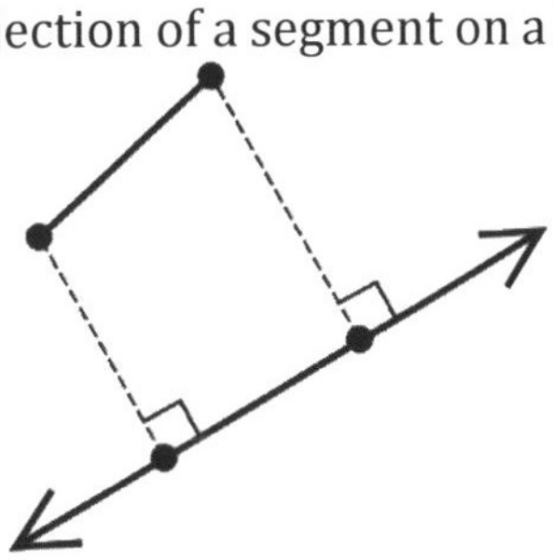

Planes

A **plane** is a two-dimensional flat surface defined by three non-collinear points. A plane extends an infinite distance in all directions in those two dimensions. It contains an infinite number of points, parallel lines and segments, intersecting lines and segments, as well as parallel or intersecting rays.

A plane will never contain a three-dimensional figure or skew lines. Two given planes are either parallel or they intersect at a line. A plane may intersect a circular conic surface to form **conic sections**, such as a parabola, hyperbola, circle or ellipse.

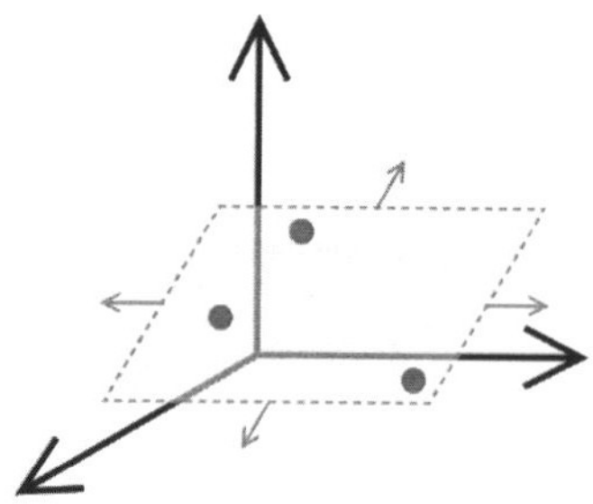

Review Video: Lines and Planes
Visit mometrix.com/academy and enter code: 554267

Angles

Angles and Vertices

An **angle** is formed when two lines or line segments meet at a common point. It may be a common starting point for a pair of segments or rays, or it may be the intersection of lines. Angles are represented by the symbol ∠.

The **vertex** is the point at which two segments or rays meet to form an angle. If the angle is formed by intersecting rays, lines, and/or line segments, the vertex is the point at which four angles are formed. The pairs of angles opposite one another are called vertical angles, and their measures are equal.

- An **acute** angle is an angle with a degree measure less than 90°.
- A **right** angle is an angle with a degree measure of exactly 90°.
- An **obtuse** angle is an angle with a degree measure greater than 90° but less than 180°.
- A **straight angle** is an angle with a degree measure of exactly 180°.
- A **reflex angle** is an angle with a degree measure greater than 180° but less than 360°.
- A **full angle** is an angle with a degree measure of exactly 360°.

Review Video: Angles
Visit mometrix.com/academy and enter code: 264624

Relationships Between Angles

Two angles whose sum is exactly 90° are said to be **complementary**. The two angles may or may not be adjacent. In a right triangle, the two acute angles are complementary.

Two angles whose sum is exactly 180° are said to be **supplementary**. The two angles may or may not be adjacent. Two intersecting lines always form two pairs of supplementary angles. Adjacent supplementary angles will always form a straight line.

Two angles that have the same vertex and share a side are said to be **adjacent**. Vertical angles are not adjacent because they share a vertex but no common side.

Review Video: Adjacent Angles
Visit mometrix.com/academy and enter code: 100375

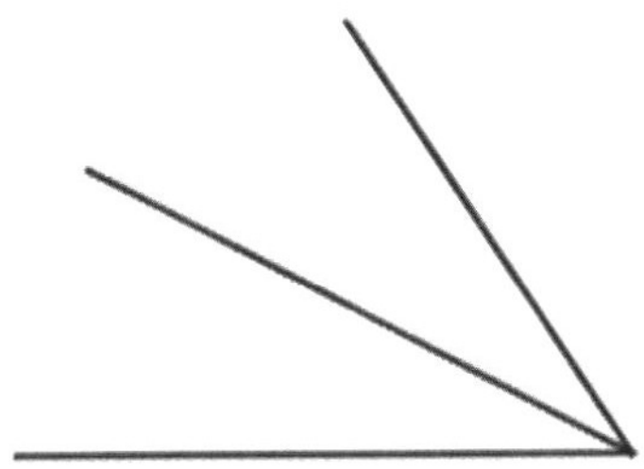

Adjacent
Share vertex and side

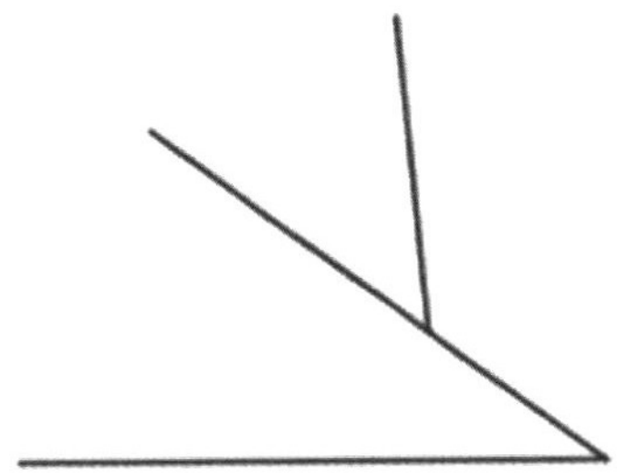

Not adjacent
Share part of a side, but not vertex

When two lines are cut by a transversal, the angles that are between the two lines are **interior angles**. In the diagram below, angles 3, 4, 5, and 6 are interior angles.

When two lines are cut by a transversal, the angles that are outside the lines are **exterior angles**. In the diagram below, angles 1, 2, 7, and 8 are exterior angles.

When two lines are cut by a transversal, the angles that are in the same position relative to the transversal and the cut lines are **corresponding angles**. The diagram below has four pairs of corresponding angles: angles 1 and 5, angles 2 and 6, angles 3 and 7, and angles 4 and 8. Corresponding angles formed by parallel lines are congruent.

When two lines are cut by a transversal, the two interior angles that are on opposite sides of the transversal are called **alternate interior angles**. In the diagram below, there are two pairs of alternate interior angles: angles 3 and 6, and angles 4 and 5. Alternate interior angles formed by parallel lines are congruent. Similarly, the two interior angles on the same side of the transversal (angles 3 and 5, and angles 4 and 6) are supplementary when the transversed lines are parallel. Some books call these angles **same side interior angles**.

When two lines are cut by a transversal, the two exterior angles that are on opposite sides of the transversal are called **alternate exterior angles**. In the diagram below, there are two pairs of alternate exterior angles: angles 1 and 8, and angles 2 and 7. Alternate exterior angles formed by parallel lines are congruent. Similarly, the two exterior angles on the same side of the transversal (angles 1 and 7, and angles 2 and 8) are supplementary when the transversed lines are parallel. Some books call these angles **same side exterior angles**.

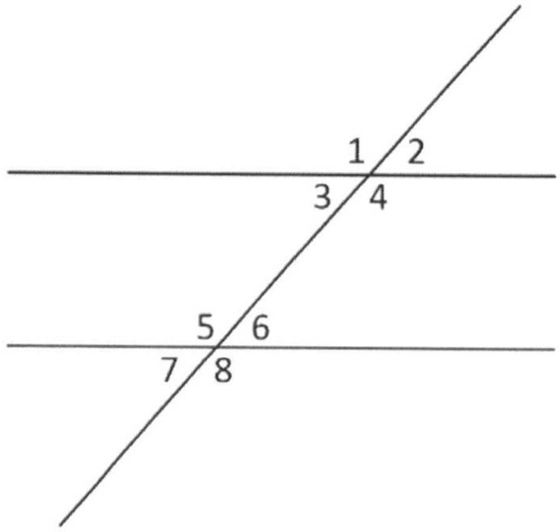

When two lines intersect, four angles are formed. The non-adjacent angles at this vertex are called vertical angles. Vertical angles are congruent. In the diagram, $\angle ABD \cong \angle CBE$ and $\angle ABC \cong \angle DBE$. The other pairs of angles, $(\angle ABC, \angle CBE)$ and $(\angle ABD, \angle DBE)$, are supplementary, meaning the pairs sum to 180°.

Review Video: Congruent Angles
Visit mometrix.com/academy and enter code: 642874

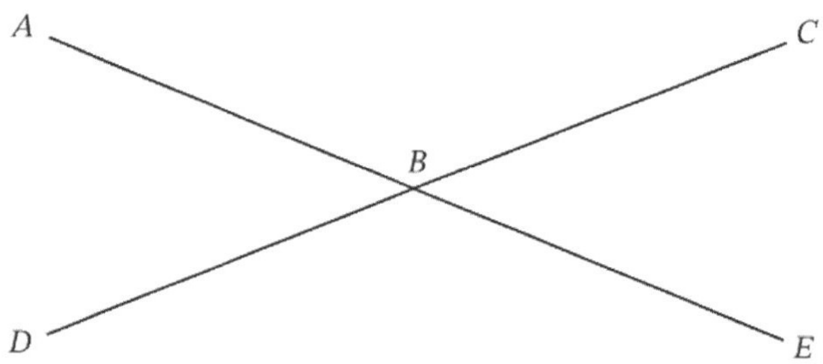

Polygons

A **polygon** is a closed, two-dimensional figure with three or more straight line segments called **sides**. The point at which two sides of a polygon intersect is called the **vertex**. In a polygon, the number of sides is always equal to the number of vertices. A polygon with all sides congruent and all angles equal is called a **regular polygon**. Common polygons are:

$$\begin{aligned} \text{Triangle} &= 3 \text{ sides} \\ \text{Quadrilateral} &= 4 \text{ sides} \\ \text{Pentagon} &= 5 \text{ sides} \\ \text{Hexagon} &= 6 \text{ sides} \\ \text{Heptagon} &= 7 \text{ sides} \\ \text{Octagon} &= 8 \text{ sides} \\ \text{Nonagon} &= 9 \text{ sides} \\ \text{Decagon} &= 10 \text{ sides} \\ \text{Dodecagon} &= 12 \text{ sides} \end{aligned}$$

More generally, an n-gon is a polygon that has n angles and n sides.

Review Video: Intro to Polygons
Visit mometrix.com/academy and enter code: 271869

The sum of the interior angles of an n-sided polygon is $(n-2) \times 180°$. For example, in a triangle $n = 3$. So the sum of the interior angles is $(3-2) \times 180° = 180°$. In a quadrilateral, $n = 4$, and the sum of the angles is $(4-2) \times 180° = 360°$.

Review Video: Sum of Interior Angles
Visit mometrix.com/academy and enter code: 984991

Convex and Concave Polygons

A **convex polygon** is a polygon whose diagonals all lie within the interior of the polygon. A **concave polygon** is a polygon with at least one diagonal that is outside the polygon. In the diagram below, quadrilateral $ABCD$ is concave because diagonal $\overline{AC}$ lies outside the polygon and quadrilateral $EFGH$ is convex because both diagonals lie inside the polygon.

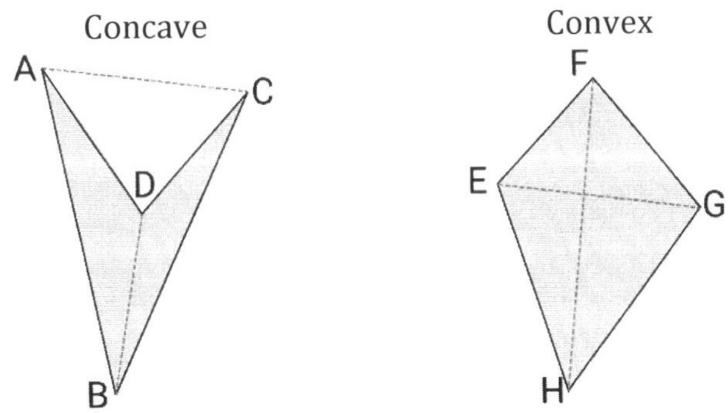

Apothem and Radius

A line segment from the center of a regular polygon that is perpendicular to a side of the polygon is called the **apothem**. A line segment from the center of a regular polygon to a vertex of the polygon is called a **radius**. In a regular polygon, the apothem can be used to find the area of the polygon using the formula $A = \frac{1}{2}ap$, where a is the apothem, and p is the perimeter.

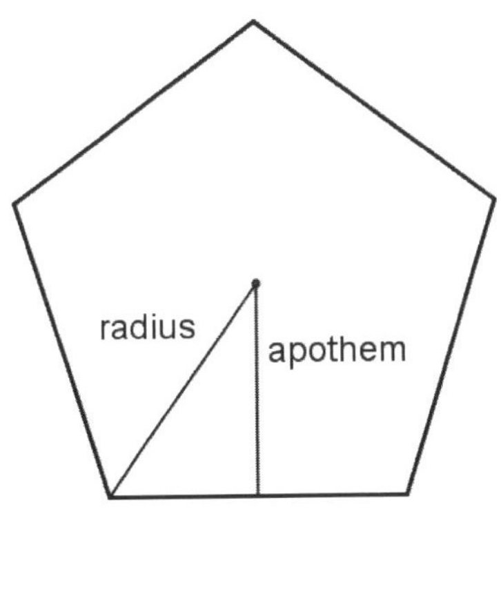

A **diagonal** is a line segment that joins two non-adjacent vertices of a polygon. The number of diagonals a polygon has can be found by using the formula:

$$\text{number of diagonals} = \frac{n(n-3)}{2}$$

Note that n is the number of sides in the polygon. This formula works for all polygons, not just regular polygons.

Congruence and Similarity

Congruent figures are geometric figures that have the same size and shape. For congruent polygons all corresponding angle measures are equal, and all corresponding side lengths are equal. Congruence is indicated by the symbol ≅. For instance, the expression $ABC \cong DEF$ indicates that the triangles below are congruent. The order of the letters is important, indicating which parts of the polygons correspond to each other. For example, since the letters A and D both come first, $\angle A$ and $\angle D$ have the same measure.

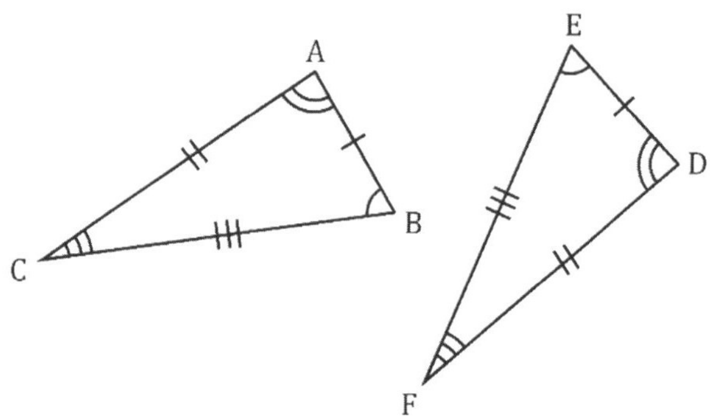

Similar figures are geometric figures that have the same shape, but do not necessarily have the same size. For similar polygons all corresponding angle measures are equal, and all corresponding side lengths are proportional, but they do not have to be equal. It is indicated by the symbol ~. For instance, the expression $ABC \sim DEF$ indicates that the triangles below are similar. Again, the order of the letters indicates which parts of the polygons correspond to each other.

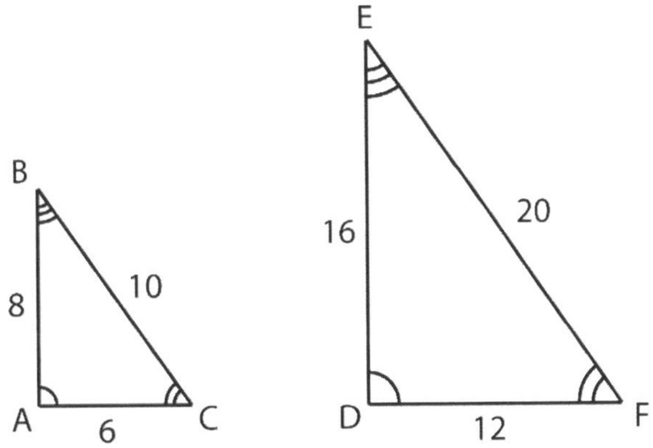

Note that all congruent figures are also similar, but not all similar figures are congruent.

Review Video: Congruent Shapes
Visit mometrix.com/academy and enter code: 492281

Line of Symmetry

A line that divides a figure or object into congruent parts that are mirror images of each other across the line is called a **line of symmetry**. An object may have no lines of symmetry, one line of symmetry, or multiple (i.e., more than one) lines of symmetry.

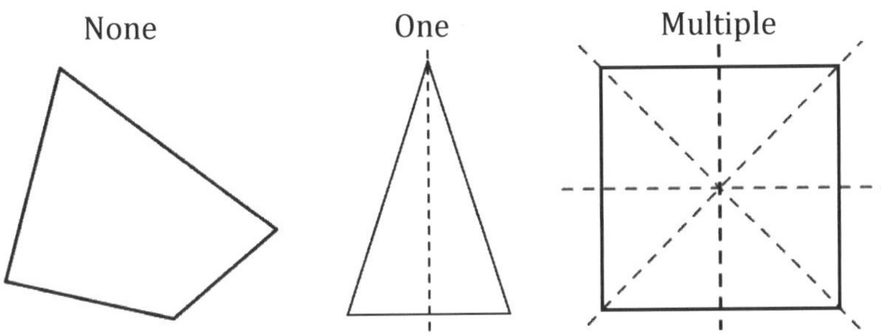

Review Video: Symmetry
Visit mometrix.com/academy and enter code: 528106

Triangles

A triangle is a three-sided figure with the sum of its interior angles being 180°. The **perimeter of any triangle** is found by summing the three side lengths; $P = a + b + c$. For an equilateral triangle, this is the same as $P = 3a$, where a is any side length, since all three sides are the same length.

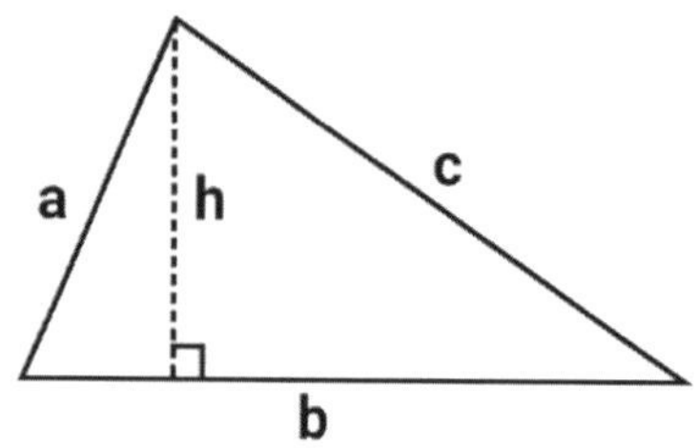

Review Video: Proof that a Triangle is 180 Degrees
Visit mometrix.com/academy and enter code: 687591

Review Video: Area and Perimeter of a Triangle
Visit mometrix.com/academy and enter code: 853779

The **area of any triangle** can be found by taking half the product of one side length referred to as the base, often given the variable b and the perpendicular distance from that side to the opposite vertex called the altitude or height and given the variable h. In equation form that is $A = \frac{1}{2}bh$. Another formula that works for any triangle is $A = \sqrt{s(s-a)(s-b)(s-c)}$, where s is the semiperimeter: $\frac{a+b+c}{2}$, and a, b, and c are the lengths of the three sides. Special cases include isosceles triangles, $A = \frac{1}{2}b\sqrt{a^2 - \frac{b^2}{4}}$, where b is the unique side and a is the length of one of the two congruent sides, and equilateral triangles, $A = \frac{\sqrt{3}}{4}a^2$, where a is the length of a side.

Review Video: Area of Any Triangle
Visit mometrix.com/academy and enter code: 138510

Parts of a Triangle

An **altitude** of a triangle is a line segment drawn from one vertex perpendicular to the opposite side. In the diagram that follows, $\overline{BE}$, $\overline{AD}$, and $\overline{CF}$ are altitudes. The length of an altitude is also called the height of the triangle. The three altitudes in a triangle are always concurrent. The point of concurrency of the altitudes of a triangle, O, is called the **orthocenter**. Note that in an obtuse triangle, the orthocenter will be outside the triangle, and in a right triangle, the orthocenter is the vertex of the right angle.

A **median** of a triangle is a line segment drawn from one vertex to the midpoint of the opposite side. In the diagram that follows, $\overline{BH}$, $\overline{AG}$, and $\overline{CI}$ are medians. This is not the same as the altitude, except the altitude to the base of an isosceles triangle and all three altitudes of an equilateral triangle. The point of concurrency of the medians of a triangle, T, is called the **centroid**. This is the same point as the orthocenter only in an equilateral triangle. Unlike the orthocenter, the centroid is always inside the triangle. The centroid can also be considered the exact center of the triangle. Any shape triangle can be perfectly balanced on a tip placed at the centroid. The centroid is also the point that is two-thirds the distance from the vertex to the opposite side.

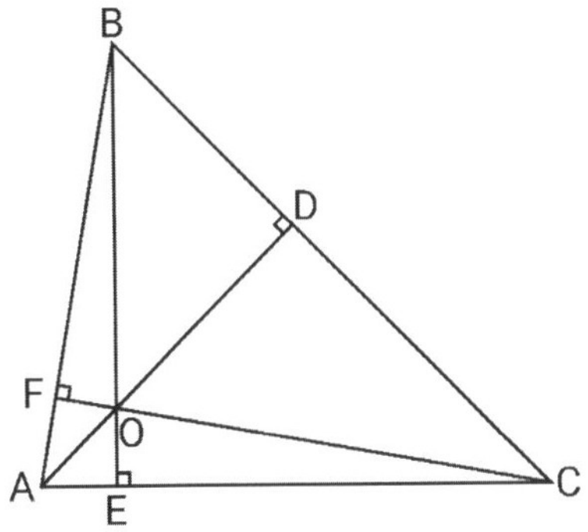

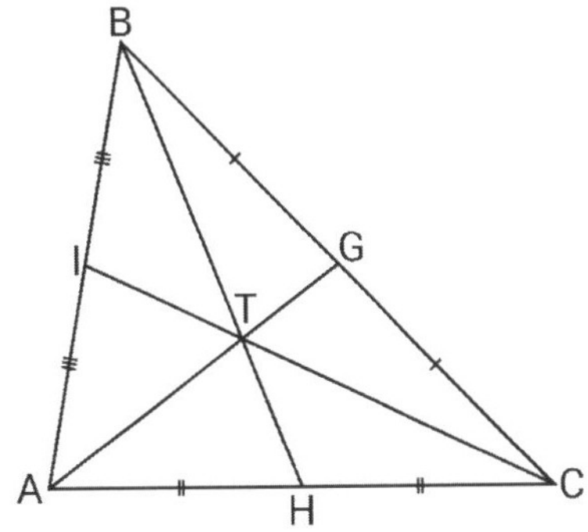

Review Video: Centroid, Incenter, Circumcenter, and Orthocenter
Visit mometrix.com/academy and enter code: 598260

Triangle Properties

Classifications of Triangles

A **scalene triangle** is a triangle with no congruent sides. A scalene triangle will also have three angles of different measures. The angle with the largest measure is opposite the longest side, and the angle with the smallest measure is opposite the shortest side. An **acute triangle** is a triangle whose three angles are all less than 90°. If two of the angles are equal, the acute triangle is also an **isosceles triangle**. An isosceles triangle will also have two congruent angles opposite the two congruent sides. If the three angles are all equal, the acute triangle is also an **equilateral triangle**. An equilateral triangle will also have three congruent angles, each 60°. All equilateral triangles are also acute triangles. An **obtuse triangle** is a triangle with exactly one angle greater than 90°. The other two angles may or may not be equal. If the two remaining angles are equal, the obtuse triangle is also an isosceles triangle. A **right triangle** is a triangle with exactly one angle equal to 90°. All right triangles follow the Pythagorean theorem. A right triangle can never be acute or obtuse.

The table below illustrates how each descriptor places a different restriction on the triangle:

Angles / Sides	**Acute: All angles < 90°**	**Obtuse: One angle > 90°**	**Right: One angle = 90°**
Scalene: No equal side lengths	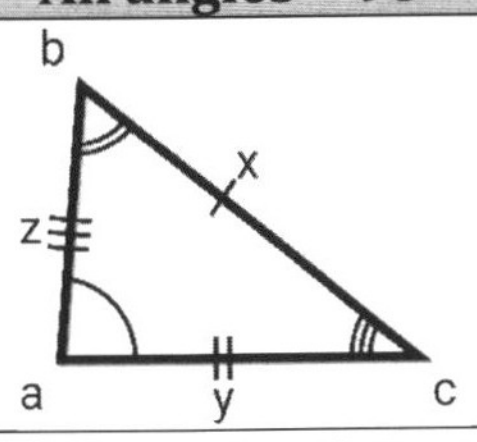	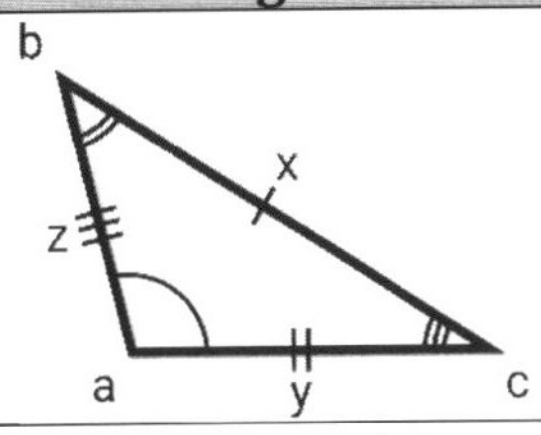	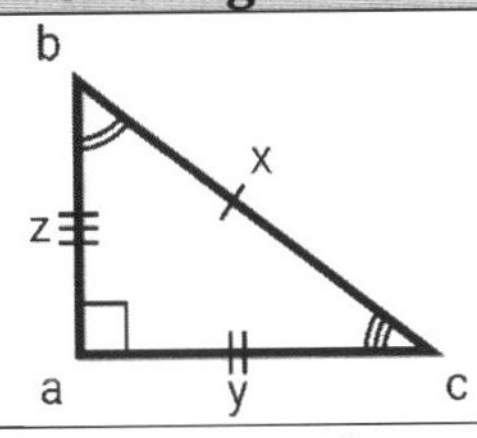
	$90° > \angle a > \angle b > \angle c$ $x > y > z$	$\angle a > 90° > \angle b > \angle c$ $x > y > z$	$90° = \angle a > \angle b > \angle c$ $x > y > z$

Angles / Sides	Acute: All angles < 90°	Obtuse: One angle > 90°	Right: One angle = 90°
Isosceles: Two equal side lengths	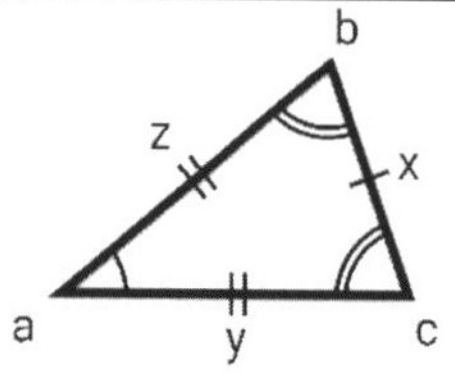	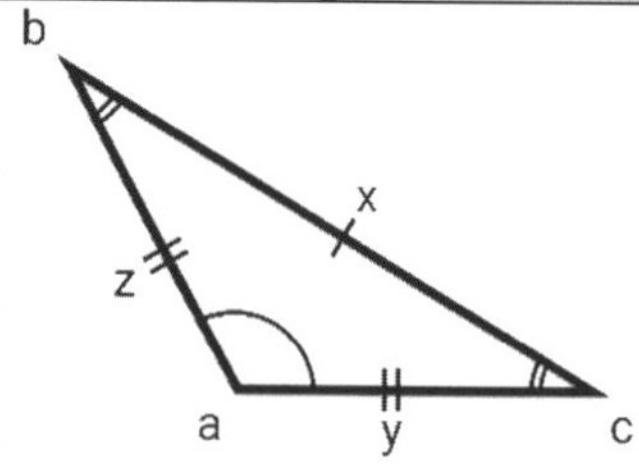	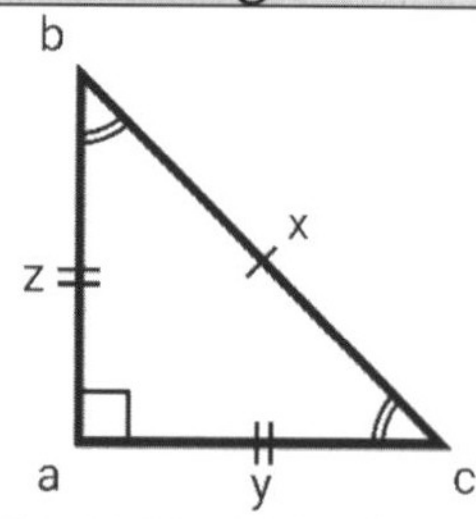
	$90° > \angle a, \angle b, or\ \angle c$ $\angle b = \angle c, \quad y = z$	$\angle a > 90° > \angle b = \angle c$ $x > y = z$	$\angle a = 90°$ $\angle b = \angle c = 45°$ $x > y = z$
Equilateral: Three equal side lengths	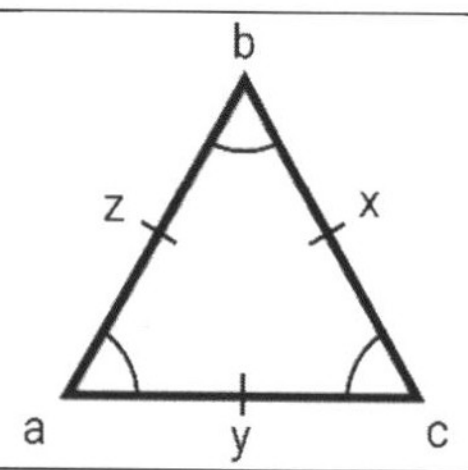		
	$60° = \angle a = \angle b = \angle c$ $x = y = z$		

Review Video: Introduction to Types of Triangles
Visit mometrix.com/academy and enter code: 511711

General Rules for Triangles

The **triangle inequality theorem** states that the sum of the measures of any two sides of a triangle is always greater than the measure of the third side. If the sum of the measures of two sides were equal to the third side, a triangle would be impossible because the two sides would lie flat across the third side and there would be no vertex. If the sum of the measures of two of the sides was less than the third side, a closed figure would be impossible because the two shortest sides would never meet. In other words, for a triangle with sides lengths A, B, and C: $A + B > C$, $B + C > A$, and $A + C > B$.

The sum of the measures of the interior angles of a triangle is always 180°. Therefore, a triangle can never have more than one angle greater than or equal to 90°.

In any triangle, the angles opposite congruent sides are congruent, and the sides opposite congruent angles are congruent. The largest angle is always opposite the longest side, and the smallest angle is always opposite the shortest side.

The line segment that joins the midpoints of any two sides of a triangle is always parallel to the third side and exactly half the length of the third side.

Review Video: General Rules (Triangle Inequality Theorem)
Visit mometrix.com/academy and enter code: 166488

Similarity and Congruence Rules

Similar triangles are triangles whose corresponding angles are equal and whose corresponding sides are proportional. Represented by AAA. Similar triangles whose corresponding sides are congruent are also congruent triangles.

Triangles can be shown to be **congruent** in 5 ways:

- **SSS**: Three sides of one triangle are congruent to the three corresponding sides of the second triangle.
- **SAS**: Two sides and the included angle (the angle formed by those two sides) of one triangle are congruent to the corresponding two sides and included angle of the second triangle.
- **ASA**: Two angles and the included side (the side that joins the two angles) of one triangle are congruent to the corresponding two angles and included side of the second triangle.
- **AAS**: Two angles and a non-included side of one triangle are congruent to the corresponding two angles and non-included side of the second triangle.
- **HL**: The hypotenuse and leg of one right triangle are congruent to the corresponding hypotenuse and leg of the second right triangle.

Review Video: Similar Triangles
Visit mometrix.com/academy and enter code: 398538

Quadrilaterals

A **quadrilateral** is a closed two-dimensional geometric figure that has four straight sides. The sum of the interior angles of any quadrilateral is 360°.

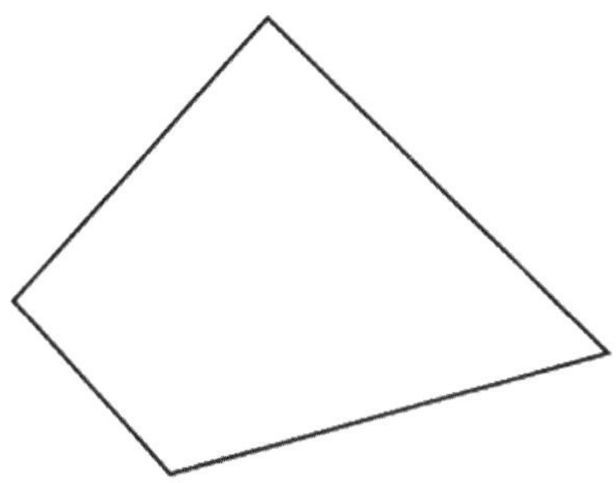

Review Video: Diagonals of Parallelograms, Rectangles, and Rhombi
Visit mometrix.com/academy and enter code: 320040

KITE

A **kite** is a quadrilateral with two pairs of adjacent sides that are congruent. A result of this is perpendicular diagonals. A kite can be concave or convex and has one line of symmetry.

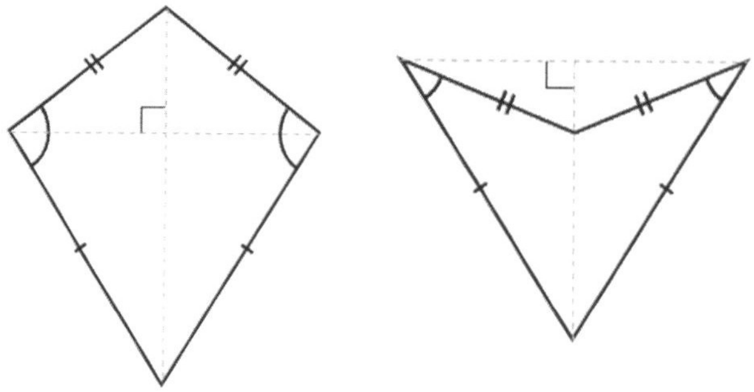

TRAPEZOID

Trapezoid: A trapezoid is defined as a quadrilateral that has at least one pair of parallel sides. There are no rules for the second pair of sides. So, there are no rules for the diagonals and no lines of symmetry for a trapezoid.

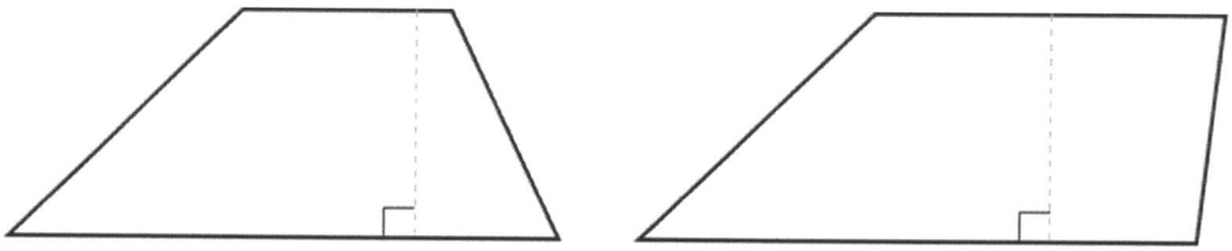

The **area of a trapezoid** is found by the formula $A = \frac{1}{2}h(b_1 + b_2)$, where h is the height (segment joining and perpendicular to the parallel bases), and b_1 and b_2 are the two parallel sides (bases). Do not use one of the other two sides as the height unless that side is also perpendicular to the parallel bases.

The **perimeter of a trapezoid** is found by the formula $P = a + b_1 + c + b_2$, where a, b_1, c, and b_2 are the four sides of the trapezoid.

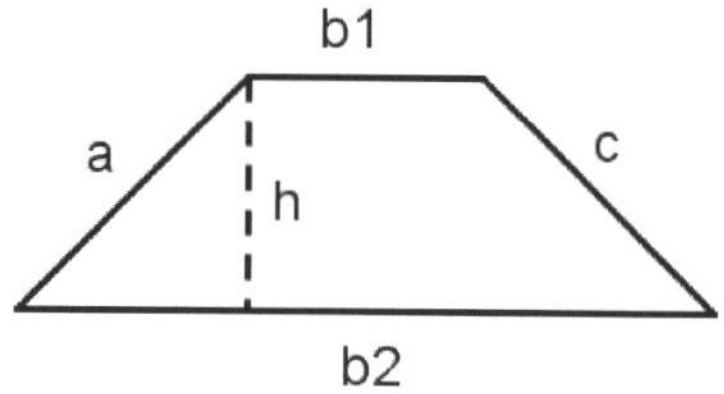

Review Video: Area and Perimeter of a Trapezoid
Visit mometrix.com/academy and enter code: 587523

Isosceles trapezoid: A trapezoid with equal base angles. This gives rise to other properties including: the two nonparallel sides have the same length, the two non-base angles are also equal, and there is one line of symmetry through the midpoints of the parallel sides.

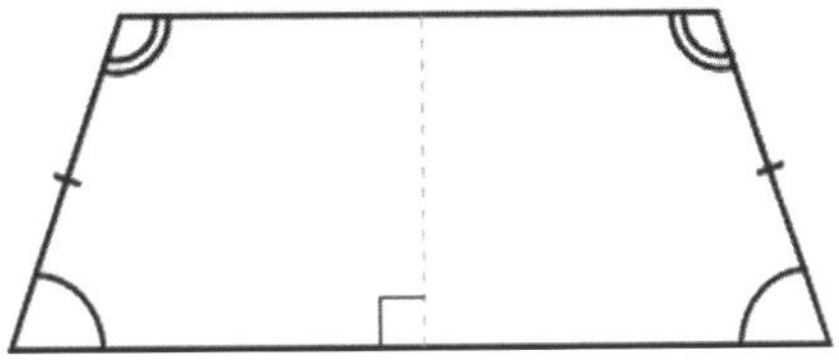

PARALLELOGRAM

A **parallelogram** is a quadrilateral that has two pairs of opposite parallel sides. As such it is a special type of trapezoid. The sides that are parallel are also congruent. The opposite interior angles are always congruent, and the consecutive interior angles are supplementary. The diagonals of a parallelogram divide each other. Each diagonal divides the parallelogram into two congruent triangles. A parallelogram has no line of symmetry, but does have 180-degree rotational symmetry about the midpoint.

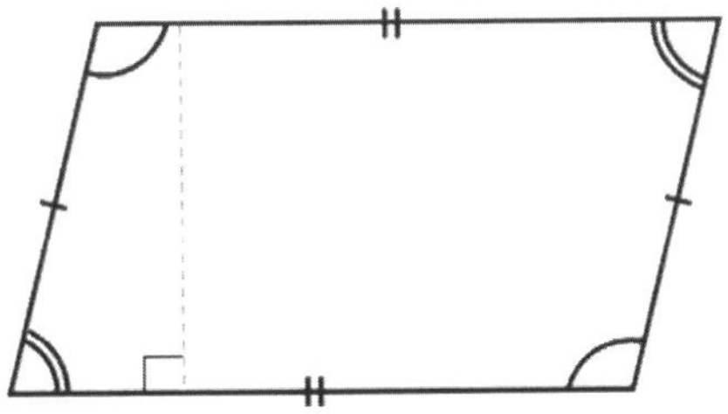

The **area of a parallelogram** is found by the formula $A = bh$, where b is the length of the base, and h is the height. Note that the base and height correspond to the length and width in a rectangle, so this formula would apply to rectangles as well. Do not confuse the height of a parallelogram with the length of the second side. The two are only the same measure in the case of a rectangle.

The **perimeter of a parallelogram** is found by the formula $P = 2a + 2b$ or $P = 2(a + b)$, where a and b are the lengths of the two sides.

Review Video: Area and Perimeter of a Parallelogram
Visit mometrix.com/academy and enter code: 718313

RECTANGLE

A **rectangle** is a quadrilateral with four right angles. All rectangles are parallelograms and trapezoids, but not all parallelograms or trapezoids are rectangles. The diagonals of a rectangle are congruent. Rectangles have two lines of symmetry (through each pair of opposing midpoints) and 180-degree rotational symmetry about the midpoint.

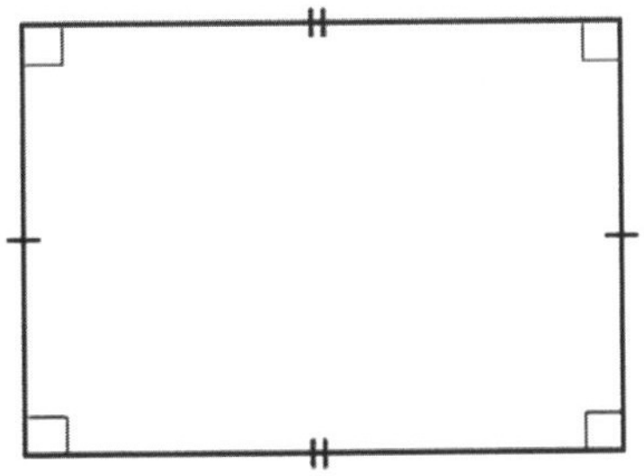

The **area of a rectangle** is found by the formula $A = lw$, where A is the area of the rectangle, l is the length (usually considered to be the longer side) and w is the width (usually considered to be the shorter side). The numbers for l and w are interchangeable.

The **perimeter of a rectangle** is found by the formula $P = 2l + 2w$ or $P = 2(l + w)$, where l is the length, and w is the width. It may be easier to add the length and width first and then double the result, as in the second formula.

RHOMBUS

A **rhombus** is a quadrilateral with four congruent sides. All rhombuses are parallelograms and kites; thus, they inherit all the properties of both types of quadrilaterals. The diagonals of a rhombus are perpendicular to each other. Rhombi have two lines of symmetry (along each of the diagonals) and 180° rotational symmetry. The **area of a rhombus** is half the product of the diagonals: $A = \frac{d_1 d_2}{2}$ and the perimeter of a rhombus is: $P = 2\sqrt{(d_1)^2 + (d_2)^2}$.

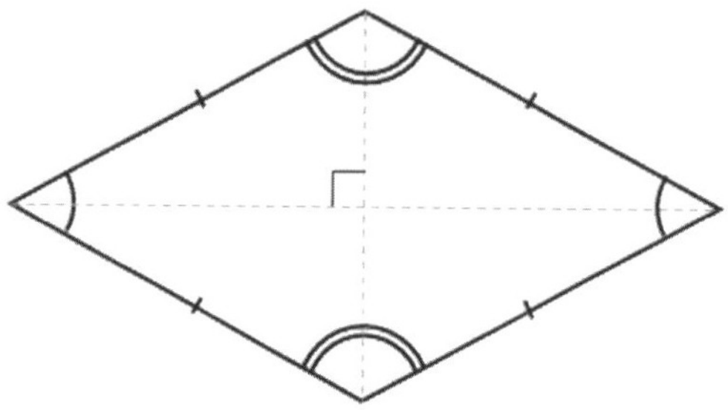

SQUARE

A **square** is a quadrilateral with four right angles and four congruent sides. Squares satisfy the criteria of all other types of quadrilaterals. The diagonals of a square are congruent and perpendicular to each other. Squares have four lines of symmetry (through each pair of opposing midpoints and along each of the diagonals) as well as 90° rotational symmetry about the midpoint.

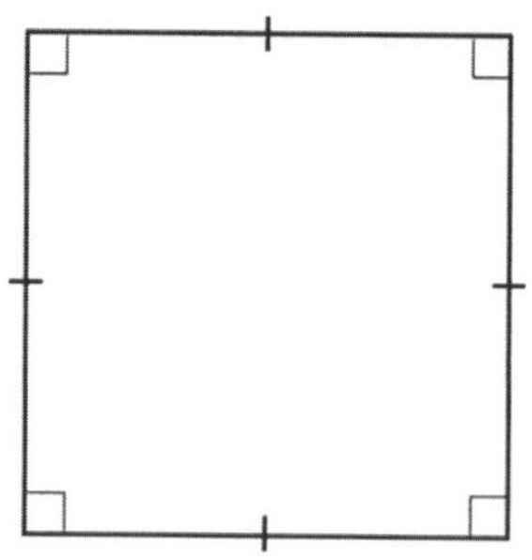

The **area of a square** is found by using the formula $A = s^2$, where s is the length of one side. The **perimeter of a square** is found by using the formula $P = 4s$, where s is the length of one side. Because all four sides are equal in a square, it is faster to multiply the length of one side by 4 than to add the same number four times. You could use the formulas for rectangles and get the same answer.

Review Video: Area and Perimeter of Rectangles and Squares
Visit mometrix.com/academy and enter code: 428109

Hierarchy of Quadrilaterals

The hierarchy of quadrilaterals is as follows:

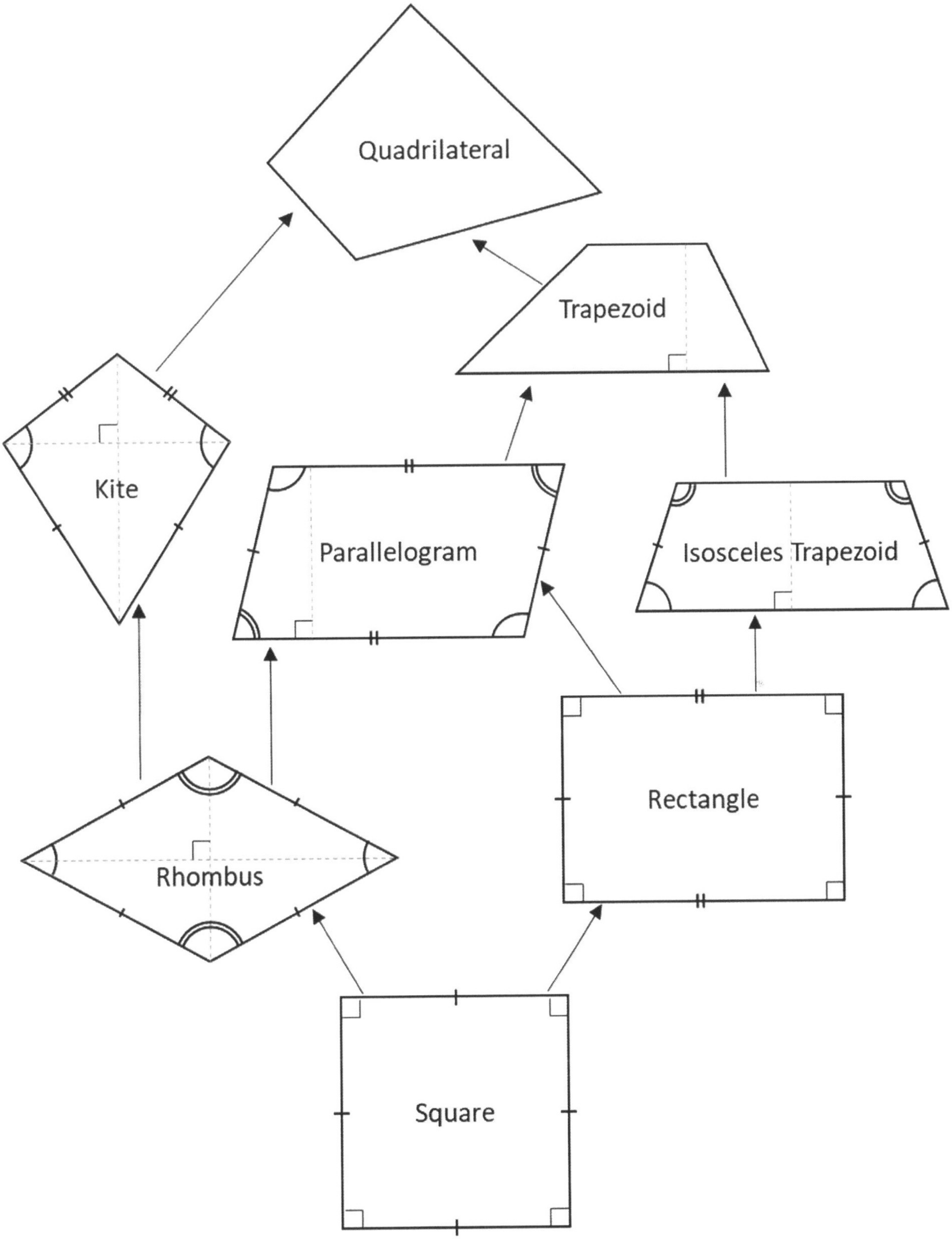

Circles

The **center** of a circle is the single point from which every point on the circle is **equidistant**. The **radius** is a line segment that joins the center of the circle and any one point on the circle. All radii of a circle are equal. Circles that have the same center but not the same length of radii are **concentric**. The **diameter** is a line segment that passes through the center of the circle and has both endpoints on the circle. The length of the diameter is exactly twice the length of the radius. Point O in the diagram below is the center of the circle, segments $\overline{OX}$, $\overline{OY}$, and $\overline{OZ}$ are radii; and segment $\overline{XZ}$ is a diameter.

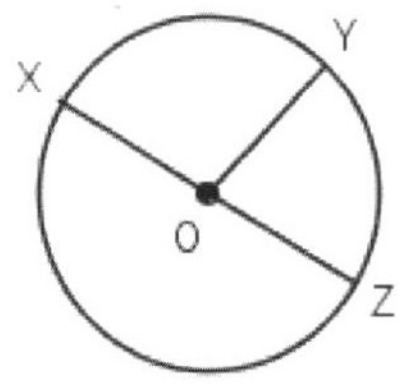

Review Video: Points of a Circle
Visit mometrix.com/academy and enter code: 420746

Review Video: Diameter, Radius, and Circumference
Visit mometrix.com/academy and enter code: 448988

The **area of a circle** is found by the formula $A = \pi r^2$, where r is the length of the radius. If the diameter of the circle is given, remember to divide it in half to get the length of the radius before proceeding.

The **circumference** of a circle is found by the formula $C = 2\pi r$, where r is the radius. Again, remember to convert the diameter if you are given that measure rather than the radius.

Review Video: Area and Circumference of a Circle
Visit mometrix.com/academy and enter code: 243015

Inscribed and Circumscribed Figures

These terms can both be used to describe a given arrangement of figures, depending on perspective. If each of the vertices of figure A lie on figure B, then it can be said that figure A is **inscribed** in figure B, but it can also be said that figure B is **circumscribed** about figure A. The following table and examples help to illustrate the concept. Note that the figures cannot both be circles, as they would be completely overlapping and neither would be inscribed or circumscribed.

Given	Description	Equivalent Description	Figures
Each of the sides of a pentagon is tangent to a circle	The circle is inscribed in the pentagon	The pentagon is circumscribed about the circle	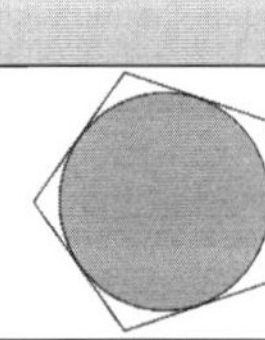
Each of the vertices of a pentagon lie on a circle	The pentagon is inscribed in the circle	The circle is circumscribed about the pentagon	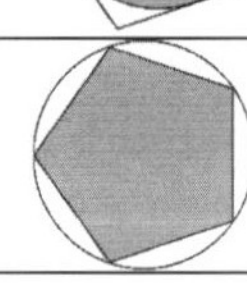

Circle Properties

Arcs

An **arc** is a portion of a circle. Specifically, an arc is the set of points between and including two points on a circle. An arc does not contain any points inside the circle. When a segment is drawn from the endpoints of an arc to the center of the circle, a sector is formed. A **minor arc** is an arc that has a measure less than 180°. A **major arc** is an arc that has a measure of at least 180°. Every minor arc has a corresponding major arc that can be found by subtracting the measure of the minor arc from 360°. A **semicircle** is an arc whose endpoints are the endpoints of the diameter of a circle. A semicircle is exactly half of a circle.

Arc length is the length of that portion of the circumference between two points on the circle. The formula for arc length is $s = \frac{\pi r \theta}{180°}$, where s is the arc length, r is the length of the radius, and θ is the angular measure of the arc in degrees, or $s = r\theta$, where θ is the angular measure of the arc in radians (2π radians $= 360$ degrees).

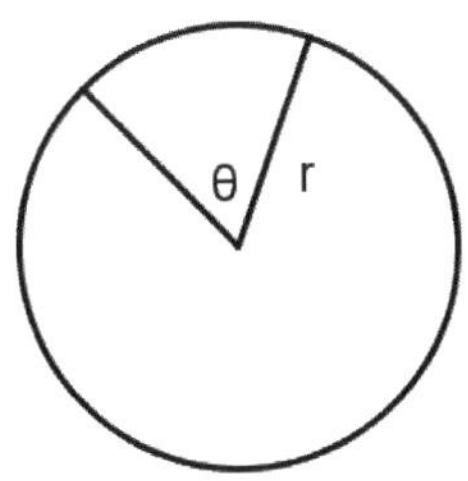

Angles of Circles

A **central angle** is an angle whose vertex is the center of a circle and whose legs intercept an arc of the circle. The measure of a central angle is equal to the measure of the minor arc it intercepts.

An **inscribed angle** is an angle whose vertex lies on a circle and whose legs contain chords of that circle. The portion of the circle intercepted by the legs of the angle is called the intercepted arc. The measure of the intercepted arc is exactly twice the measure of the inscribed angle. In the following diagram, angle ABC is an inscribed angle. $\widehat{AC} = 2(\text{m}\angle ABC)$.

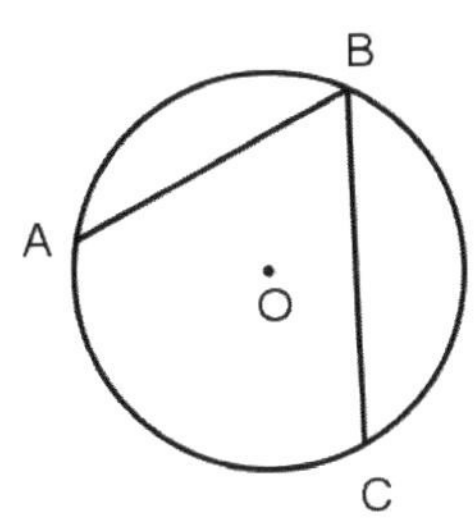

Any angle inscribed in a semicircle is a right angle. The intercepted arc is 180°, making the inscribed angle half that, or 90°. In the diagram below, angle ABC is inscribed in semicircle ABC, making angle ABC equal to 90°.

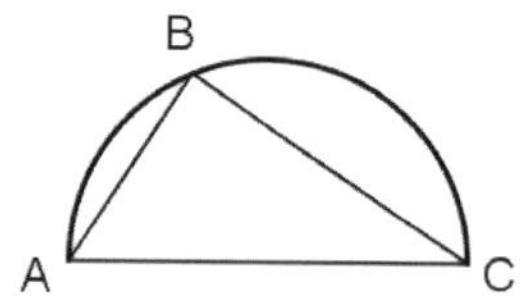

Review Video: Arcs and Angles of Circles
Visit mometrix.com/academy and enter code: 652838

SECANTS, CHORDS, AND TANGENTS

A **secant** is a line that intersects a circle in two points. The segment of a secant line that is contained within the circle is called a **chord**. Two secants may intersect inside the circle, on the circle, or outside the circle. When the two secants intersect on the circle, an inscribed angle is formed. When two secants intersect inside a circle, the measure of each of two vertical angles is equal to half the sum of the two intercepted arcs. Consider the following diagram where $\text{m}\angle AEB = \frac{1}{2}(\widehat{AB} + \widehat{CD})$ and $\text{m}\angle BEC = \frac{1}{2}(\widehat{BC} + \widehat{AD})$.

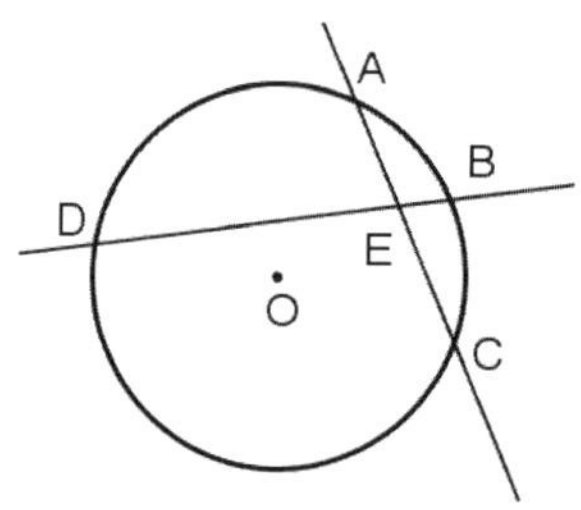

When two secants intersect outside a circle, the measure of the angle formed is equal to half the difference of the two arcs that lie between the two secants. In the diagram below, $\text{m}\angle AEB = \frac{1}{2}(\widehat{AB} - \widehat{CD})$.

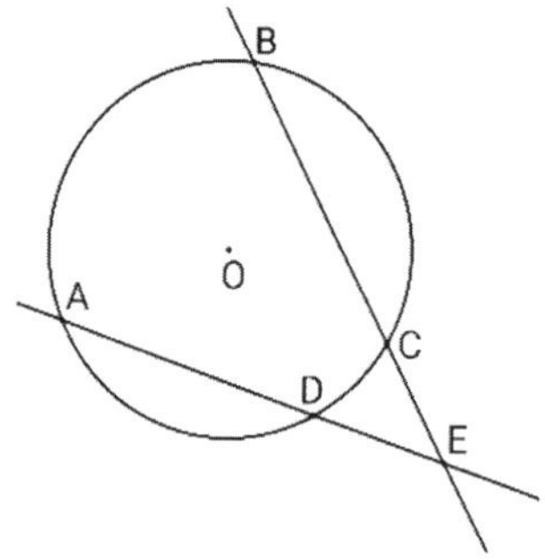

A **tangent** is a line in the same plane as a circle that touches the circle in exactly one point. The point at which a tangent touches a circle is called the **point of tangency**. While a line segment can be tangent to a circle as part of a line that is tangent, it is improper to say a tangent can be simply a line segment that touches the circle in exactly one point.

In the diagram below, $\overleftrightarrow{EB}$ is a secant and contains chord $\overline{EB}$, and $\overleftrightarrow{CD}$ is tangent to circle A. Notice that $\overline{FB}$ is not tangent to the circle. $\overline{FB}$ is a line segment that touches the circle in exactly one point, but if the segment were extended, it would touch the circle in a second point. In the diagram below, point B is the point of tangency.

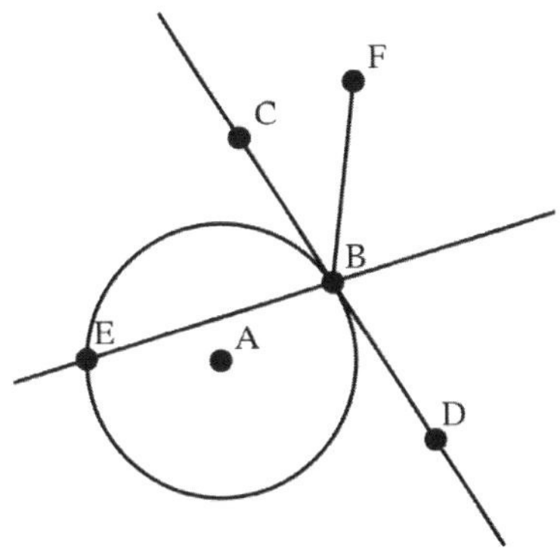

Review Video: Secants, Chords, and Tangents
Visit mometrix.com/academy and enter code: 258360

Review Video: Tangent Lines of a Circle
Visit mometrix.com/academy and enter code: 780167

Sectors

A **sector** is the portion of a circle formed by two radii and their intercepted arc. While the arc length is exclusively the points that are also on the circumference of the circle, the sector is the entire area bounded by the arc and the two radii.

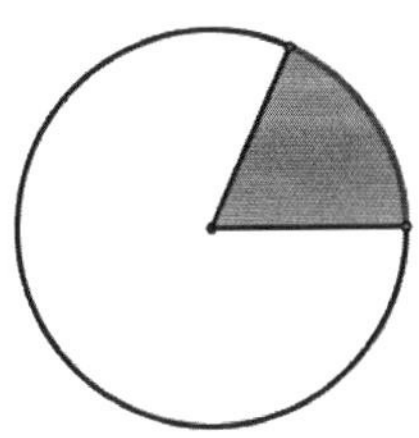

The **area of a sector** of a circle is found by the formula, $A = \frac{\theta r^2}{2}$, where A is the area, θ is the measure of the central angle in radians, and r is the radius. To find the area with the central angle in degrees, use the formula, $A = \frac{\theta \pi r^2}{360}$, where θ is the measure of the central angle and r is the radius.

Transformations

Rotation

A **rotation** is a transformation that turns a figure around a point called the **center of rotation**, which can lie anywhere in the plane. If a line is drawn from a point on a figure to the center of rotation, and another line is drawn from the center to the rotated image of that point, the angle between the two lines is the **angle of rotation**. The vertex of the angle of rotation is the center of rotation.

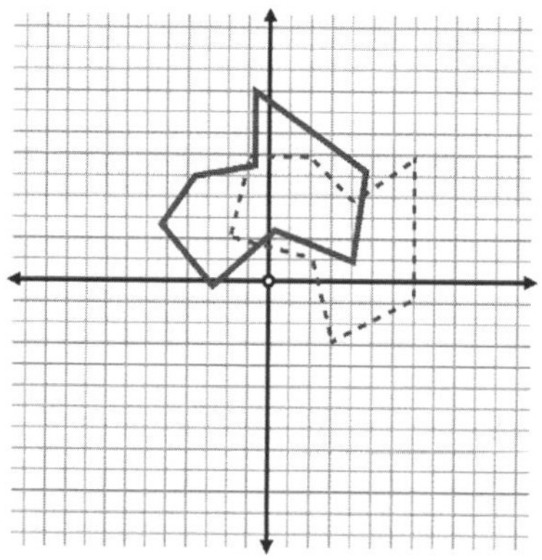

Review Video: Rotation
Visit mometrix.com/academy and enter code: 602600

Translation and Dilation

A **translation** is a transformation which slides a figure from one position in the plane to another position in the plane. The original figure and the translated figure have the same size, shape, and orientation. A **dilation** is a transformation which proportionally stretches or shrinks a figure by a **scale factor**. The dilated image is the same shape and orientation as the original image but a different size. A polygon and its dilated image are similar.

Translation

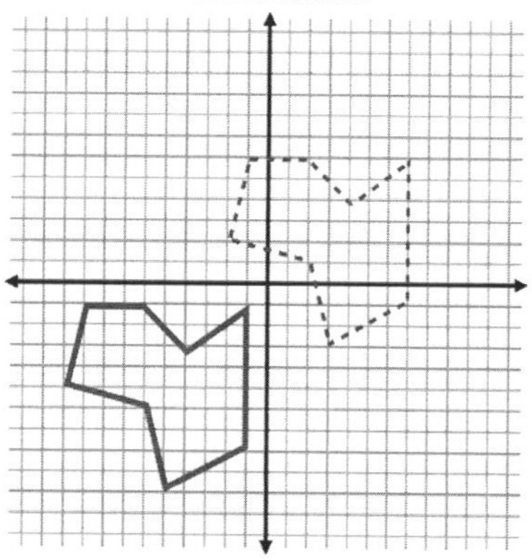

Dilation

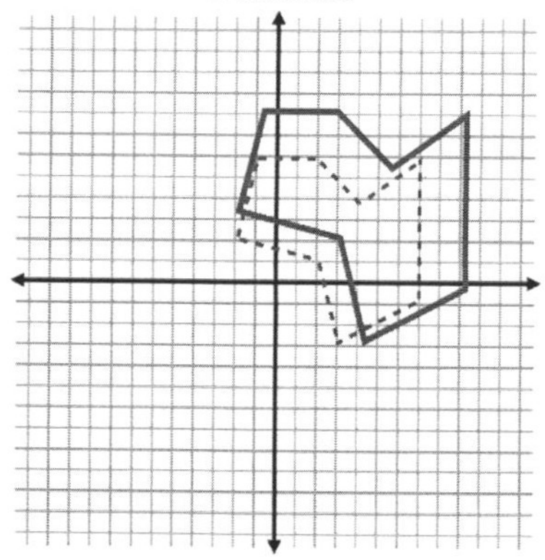

Review Video: Translation
Visit mometrix.com/academy and enter code: 718628

Review Video: Dilation
Visit mometrix.com/academy and enter code: 471630

A **reflection of a figure over a line** (a "flip") creates a congruent image that is the same distance from the line as the original figure but on the opposite side. The **line of reflection** is the perpendicular bisector of any line segment drawn from a point on the original figure to its reflected image (unless the point and its reflected image happen to be the same point, which happens when a figure is reflected over one of its own sides). A **reflection of a figure over a point** (an inversion) in two dimensions is the same as the rotation of the figure 180° about that point. The image of the figure is congruent to the original figure. The **point of reflection** is the midpoint of a line segment which connects a point in the figure to its image (unless the point and its reflected image happen to be the same point, which happens when a figure is reflected in one of its own points).

Reflection of a figure over a line

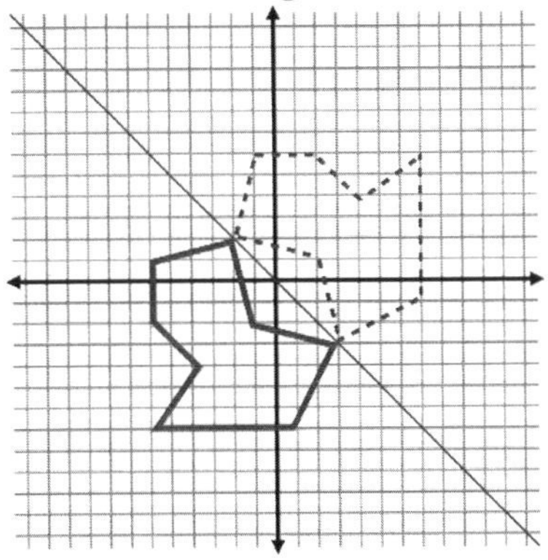

Reflection of a figure over a point

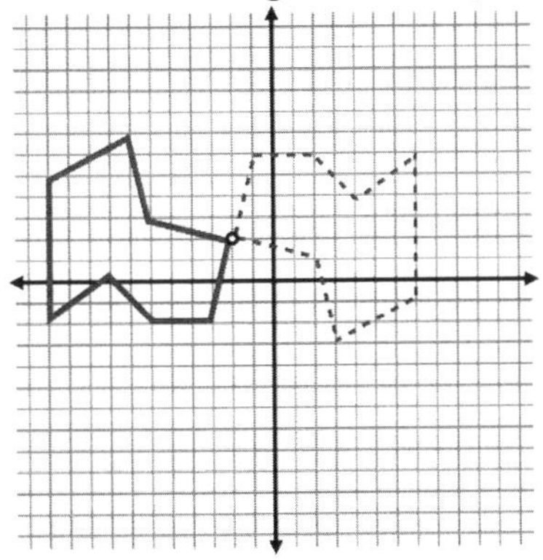

Review Video: <u>**Reflection**</u>
Visit mometrix.com/academy and enter code: 955068

3D Shapes

Solids

The **surface area of a solid object** is the area of all sides or exterior surfaces. For objects such as prisms and pyramids, a further distinction is made between base surface area (B) and lateral surface area (LA). For a prism, the total surface area (SA) is $SA = LA + 2B$. For a pyramid or cone, the total surface area is $SA = LA + B$.

The **surface area of a sphere** can be found by the formula $A = 4\pi r^2$, where r is the radius. The volume is given by the formula $V = \frac{4}{3}\pi r^3$, where r is the radius. Both quantities are generally given in terms of π.

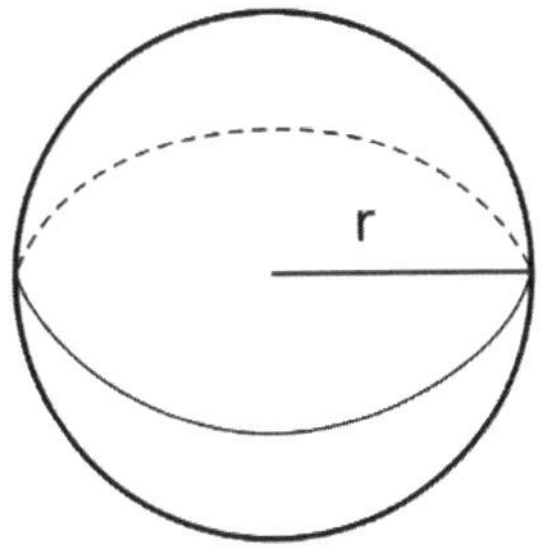

Review Video: <u>**Volume and Surface Area of a Sphere**</u>
Visit mometrix.com/academy and enter code: 786928

Review Video: <u>**How to Calculate the Volume of 3D Objects**</u>
Visit mometrix.com/academy and enter code: 163343

The **volume of any prism** is found by the formula $V = Bh$, where B is the area of the base, and h is the height (perpendicular distance between the bases). The surface area of any prism is the sum of the areas of both bases and all sides. It can be calculated as $SA = 2B + Ph$, where P is the perimeter of the base.

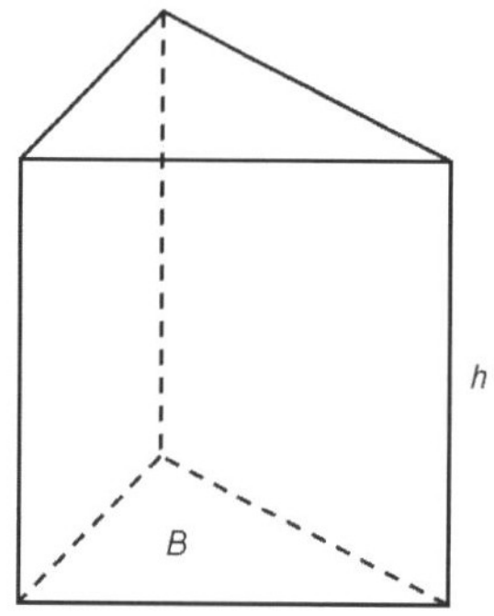

Review Video: Volume and Surface Area of a Prism
Visit mometrix.com/academy and enter code: 420158

For a **rectangular prism**, the volume can be found by the formula $V = lwh$, where V is the volume, l is the length, w is the width, and h is the height. The surface area can be calculated as $SA = 2lw + 2hl + 2wh$ or $SA = 2(lw + hl + wh)$.

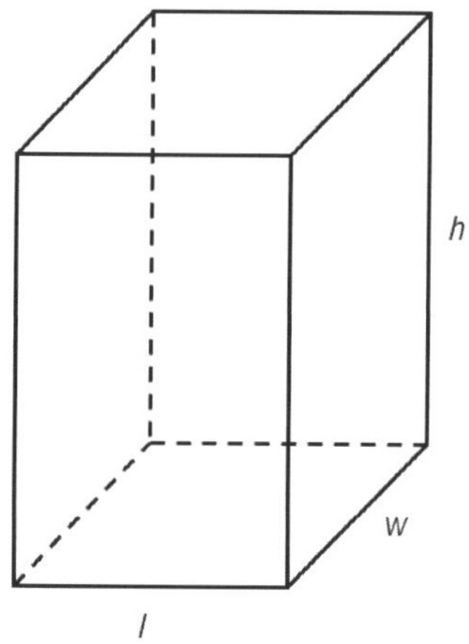

Review Video: Volume and Surface Area of a Rectangular Prism
Visit mometrix.com/academy and enter code: 282814

The **volume of a cube** can be found by the formula $V = s^3$, where s is the length of a side. The surface area of a cube is calculated as $SA = 6s^2$, where SA is the total surface area and s is the length of a side. These formulas are the same as the ones used for the volume and surface area of a rectangular prism, but simplified since all three quantities (length, width, and height) are the same.

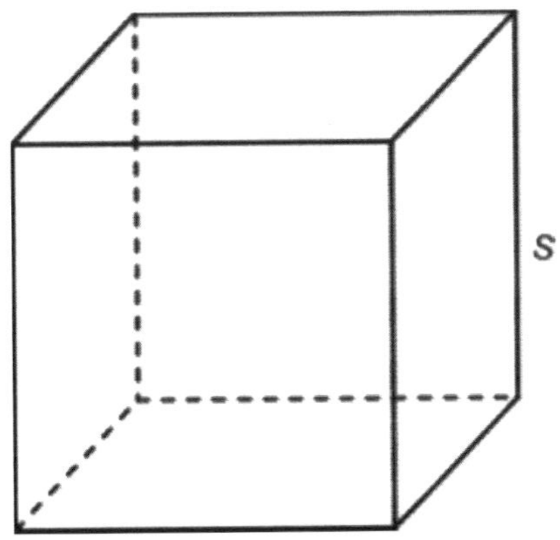

Review Video: Volume and Surface Area of a Cube
Visit mometrix.com/academy and enter code: 664455

The **volume of a cylinder** can be calculated by the formula $V = \pi r^2 h$, where r is the radius, and h is the height. The surface area of a cylinder can be found by the formula $SA = 2\pi r^2 + 2\pi rh$. The first term is the base area multiplied by two, and the second term is the perimeter of the base multiplied by the height.

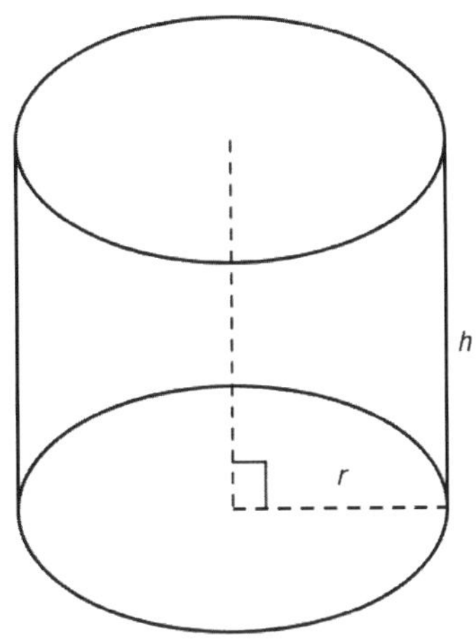

Review Video: Volume and Surface Area of a Right Circular Cylinder
Visit mometrix.com/academy and enter code: 226463

The **volume of a pyramid** is found by the formula $V = \frac{1}{3}Bh$, where B is the area of the base, and h is the height (perpendicular distance from the vertex to the base). Notice this formula is the same as $\frac{1}{3}$ times the volume of a prism. Like a prism, the base of a pyramid can be any shape.

Finding the **surface area of a pyramid** is not as simple as the other shapes we've looked at thus far. If the pyramid is a right pyramid, meaning the base is a regular polygon and the vertex is directly over the center of that polygon, the surface area can be calculated as $SA = B + \frac{1}{2}Ph_s$, where P is the perimeter of the base, and h_s is the slant height (distance from the vertex to the midpoint of one side of the base). If the pyramid is irregular, the area of each triangle side must be calculated individually and then summed, along with the base.

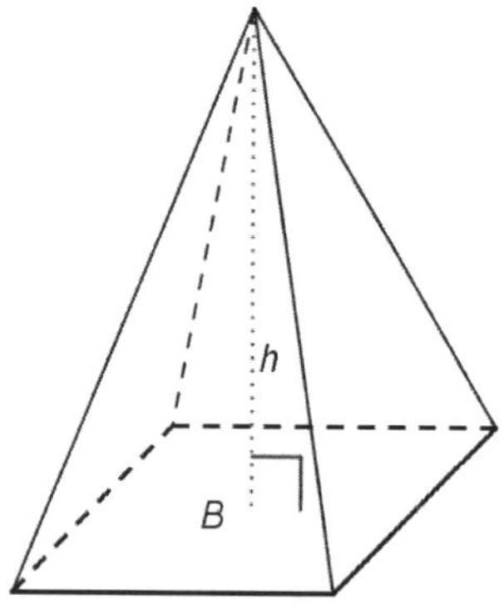

Review Video: Volume and Surface Area of a Pyramid
Visit mometrix.com/academy and enter code: 621932

The **volume of a cone** is found by the formula $V = \frac{1}{3}\pi r^2 h$, where r is the radius, and h is the height. Notice this is the same as $\frac{1}{3}$ times the volume of a cylinder. The surface area can be calculated as $SA = \pi r^2 + \pi rs$, where s is the slant height. The slant height can be calculated using the Pythagorean theorem to be $\sqrt{r^2 + h^2}$, so the surface area formula can also be written as $SA = \pi r^2 + \pi r\sqrt{r^2 + h^2}$.

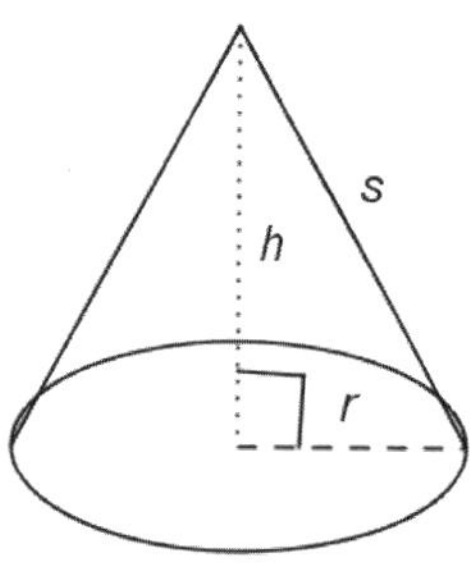

Review Video: Volume and Surface Area of a Right Circular Cone
Visit mometrix.com/academy and enter code: 573574

Pythagorean Theorem

The side of a triangle opposite the right angle is called the **hypotenuse**. The other two sides are called the legs. The Pythagorean theorem states a relationship among the legs and hypotenuse of a right triangle: $(a^2 + b^2 = c^2)$, where a and b are the lengths of the legs of a right triangle, and c is the length of the hypotenuse. Note that this formula will only work with right triangles.

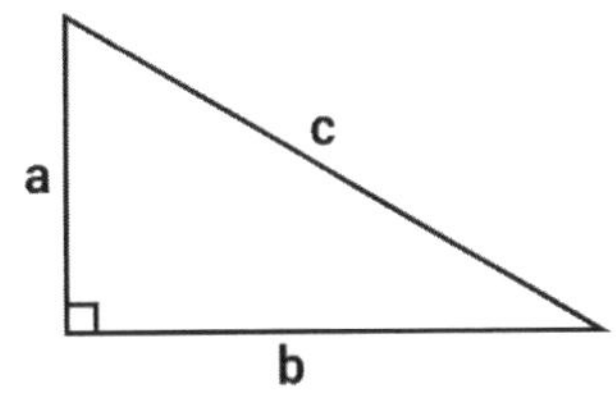

Review Video: Pythagorean Theorem
Visit mometrix.com/academy and enter code: 906576

Trigonometric Formulas

In the diagram below, angle C is the right angle, and side c is the hypotenuse. Side a is the side opposite to angle A and side b is the side opposite to angle B. Using ratios of side lengths as a means to calculate the sine, cosine, and tangent of an acute angle only works for right triangles.

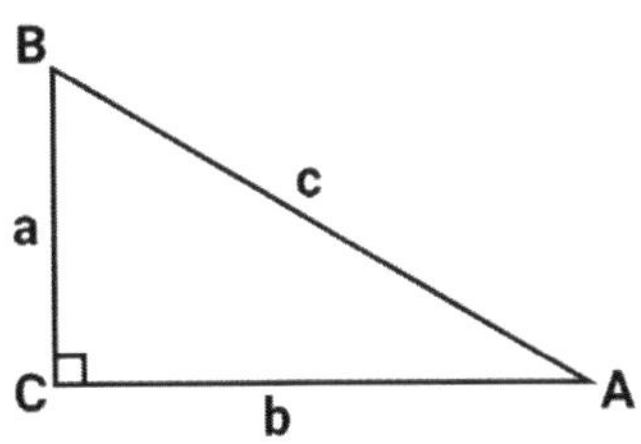

$$\sin A = \frac{\text{opposite side}}{\text{hypotenuse}} = \frac{a}{c} \qquad \csc A = \frac{1}{\sin A} = \frac{\text{hypotenuse}}{\text{opposite side}} = \frac{c}{a}$$

$$\cos A = \frac{\text{adjacent side}}{\text{hypotenuse}} = \frac{b}{c} \qquad \sec A = \frac{1}{\cos A} = \frac{\text{hypotenuse}}{\text{adjacent side}} = \frac{c}{b}$$

$$\tan A = \frac{\text{opposite side}}{\text{adjacent side}} = \frac{a}{b} \qquad \cot A = \frac{1}{\tan A} = \frac{\text{adjacent side}}{\text{opposite side}} = \frac{b}{a}$$

Laws of Sines and Cosines

The **law of sines** states that $\frac{\sin A}{a} = \frac{\sin B}{b} = \frac{\sin C}{c}$, where A, B, and C are the angles of a triangle, and a, b, and c are the sides opposite their respective angles. This formula will work with all triangles, not just right triangles.

The **law of cosines** is given by the formula $c^2 = a^2 + b^2 - 2ab(\cos C)$, where a, b, and c are the sides of a triangle, and C is the angle opposite side c. This is a generalized form of the Pythagorean theorem that can be used on any triangle.

Review Video: Law of Sines
Visit mometrix.com/academy and enter code: 206844

Review Video: Law of Cosines
Visit mometrix.com/academy and enter code: 158911

Ellipses and Hyperbolas

Ellipse

An **ellipse** is the set of all points in a plane whose total distance from two fixed points called the **foci** (singular: focus) is constant, and whose center is the midpoint between the foci.

The standard equation of an ellipse that is wider than it is tall is $\frac{(x-h)^2}{a^2} + \frac{(y-k)^2}{b^2} = 1$, where a and b are coefficients. The center is the point (h, k) and the foci are the points $(h + c, k)$ and $(h - c, k)$, where $c^2 = a^2 - b^2$ and $a^2 > b^2$.

The major axis has length $2a$, and the minor axis has length $2b$.

Eccentricity (e) is a measure of how elongated an ellipse is, and is the ratio of the distance between the foci to the length of the major axis. Eccentricity will have a value between 0 and 1. The closer to 0 the eccentricity is, the closer the ellipse is to being a circle. The formula for eccentricity is $e = \frac{c}{a}$.

Review Video: Ellipse
Visit mometrix.com/academy and enter code: 703899

Hyperbola

A **hyperbola** is the set of all points in a plane, whose distance from two fixed points, called foci, has a constant difference.

The standard equation of a horizontal hyperbola is $\frac{(x-h)^2}{a^2} - \frac{(y-k)^2}{b^2} = 1$, where $a, b, h,$ and k are real numbers. The center is the point (h, k), the vertices are the points $(h + a, k)$ and $(h - a, k)$, and the foci are the points that every point on one of the parabolic curves is equidistant from. The foci are found using the formulas $(h + c, k)$ and $(h - c, k)$, where $c^2 = a^2 + b^2$. The asymptotes are two lines the graph of the hyperbola approaches but never reaches, and are given by the equations $y = \left(\frac{b}{a}\right)(x - h) + k$ and $y = -\left(\frac{b}{a}\right)(x - h) + k$.

The standard equation of a vertical hyperbola is $\frac{(y-k)^2}{a^2} - \frac{(x-h)^2}{b^2} = 1$, where $a, b, k,$ and h are real numbers. The center is the point (h, k), the vertices are the points $(h, k + a)$ and $(h, k - a)$, and the foci are the points that every point on one of the hyperbolic curves is equidistant from and are found using the formulas $(h, k + c)$ and $(h, k - c)$, where $c^2 = a^2 + b^2$. The asymptotes are two lines the graph of the hyperbola approaches but never reaches, and are given by the equations $y = \left(\frac{a}{b}\right)(x - h) + k$ and $y = -\left(\frac{a}{b}\right)(x - h) + k$.

Review Video: Hyperbolas
Visit mometrix.com/academy and enter code: 509429

Conic Sections

Conic sections are a family of shapes that can be thought of as cross sections of a pair of infinite right cones stacked vertex to vertex. This is easiest to see with a visual representation:

A three-dimensional look at representative conic sections. (Note that a hyperbola intersects both cones.)

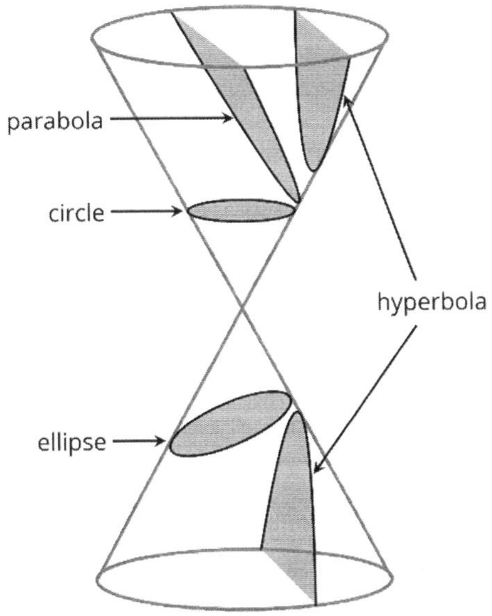

A side-on look at representative conic sections. (Note that the parabola is parallel to the slant of the cones.)

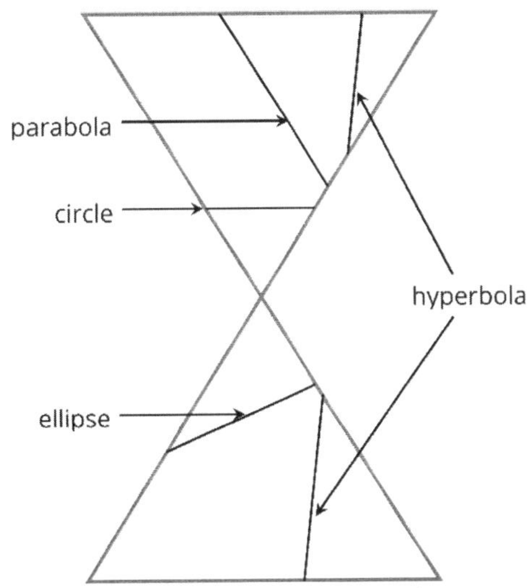

In short, a circle is a horizontal cross section, a parabola is a cross section parallel to the slant of the cone, an ellipse is a cross section at an angle *less than* the slant of the cone, and a hyperbola is a cross section at an angle *greater than* the slant of the cone.

Chapter Quiz

Ready to see how well you retained what you just read? Scan the QR code to go directly to the chapter quiz interface for this study guide. If you're using a computer, simply visit the online resources page at **mometrix.com/resources719/ssreggeometry** and click the Chapter Quizzes link.

Regents Practice Test #1

Want to take this practice test in an online interactive format?
Check out the online resources page, which includes interactive practice questions and much more: **mometrix.com/resources719/ssreggeometry**

For questions 1–25, select the best answer from the answer choices.

1. In the figure below, what is the measure of $\angle X$?

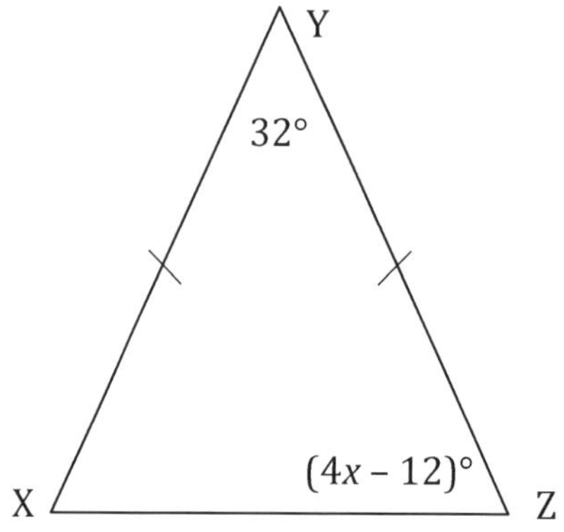

a. 32°
b. 64°
c. 74°
d. 148°

2. In triangle *ABC* below, segments *AF*, *BD*, and *CE* are the medians, intersecting at the centroid *G*. If $CE = 6x - 9$ and $CG = 2x + 3$, what is the length of *GE*?

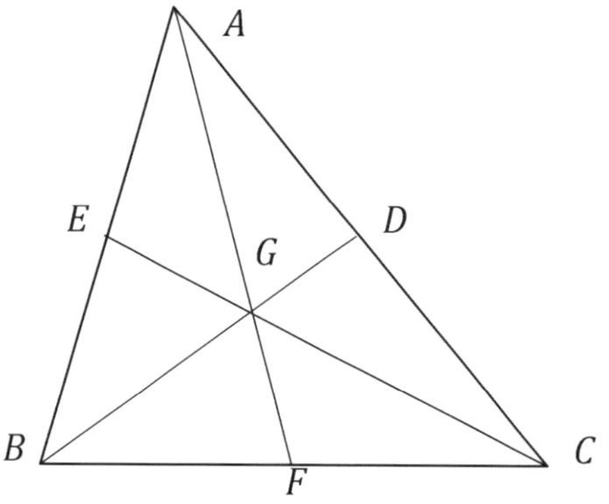

a. 4.5
b. 6
c. 12
d. 18

3. In the figure shown below, *ABCD* is a parallelogram. What is the measure of ∠*DCB*?

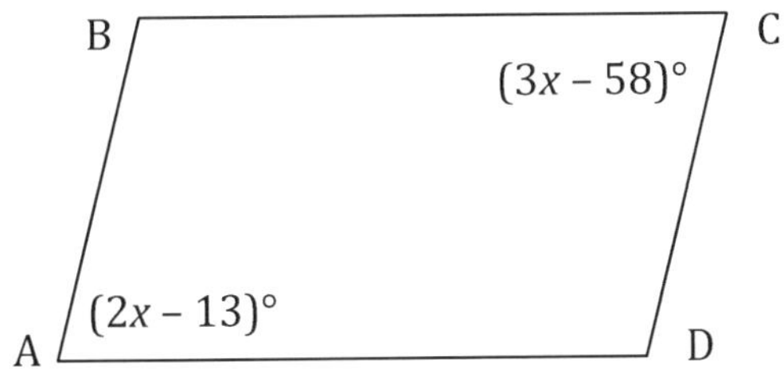

a. 38.6°
b. 45°
c. 77°
d. 92.6°

4. Which of the following statements is the definition of perpendicular lines?

a. Two distinct coplanar lines that intersect at a 90°angle.
b. Two distinct coplanar lines that do not intersect.
c. Two rays with a common endpoint that point in opposite directions.
d. Two rays sharing a common endpoint.

5. Given the line $y = -\frac{3}{4}x + 1$, find the equation of a line perpendicular to that line that passes through the point (0, 6).

a. $y = \frac{3}{4}x + 6$
b. $y = -\frac{3}{4}x + 6$
c. $y = -\frac{4}{3}x + 6$
d. $y = \frac{4}{3}x + 6$

6. In the figure below, lines *a* and *b* are parallel. Find the value of *x*.

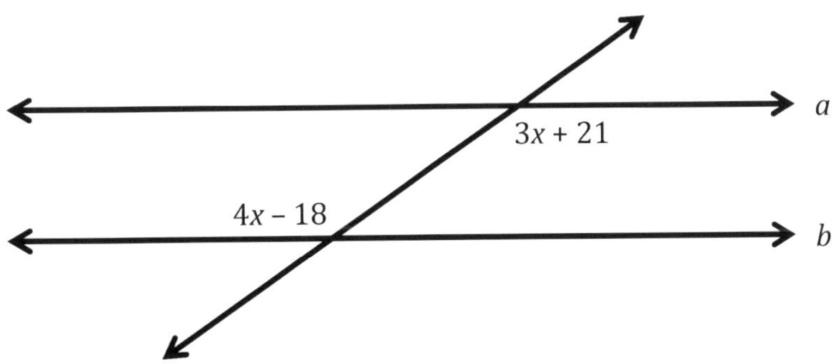

a. $x = \frac{87}{7}$
b. $x = \frac{177}{7}$
c. $x = 39$
d. $x = 138$

7. If triangle ABC, shown below, was rotated 270° clockwise about the origin, determine which notation would represent the new coordinates of $A'B'C'$?

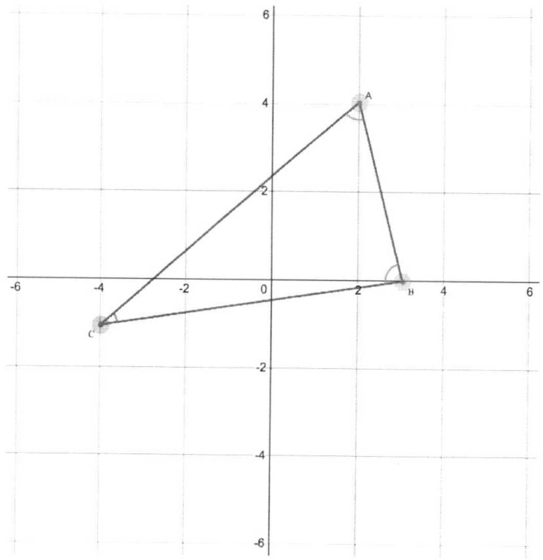

a. $(x, y) \rightarrow (-x, -y)$
b. $(x, y) \rightarrow (y, -x)$
c. $(x, y) \rightarrow (-y, x)$
d. $(x, y) \rightarrow (y, x)$

8. Which set of figures is congruent?

a. 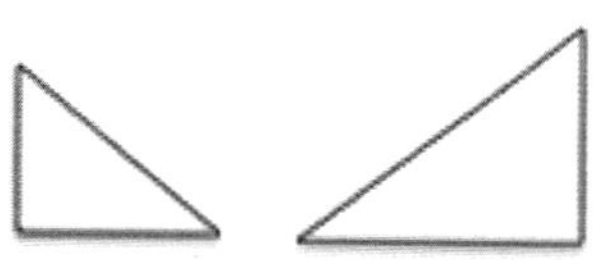

b. 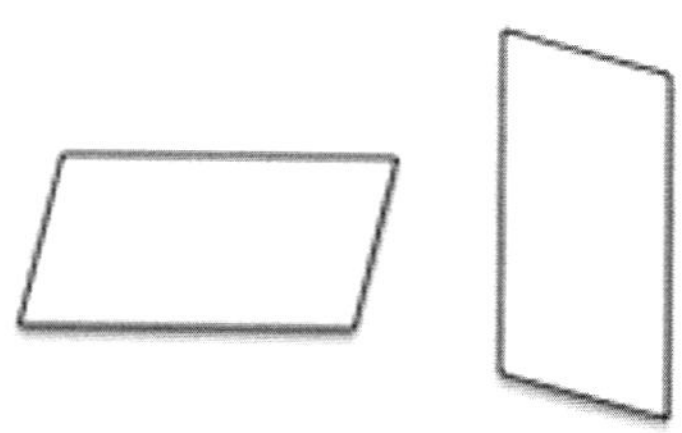

c. 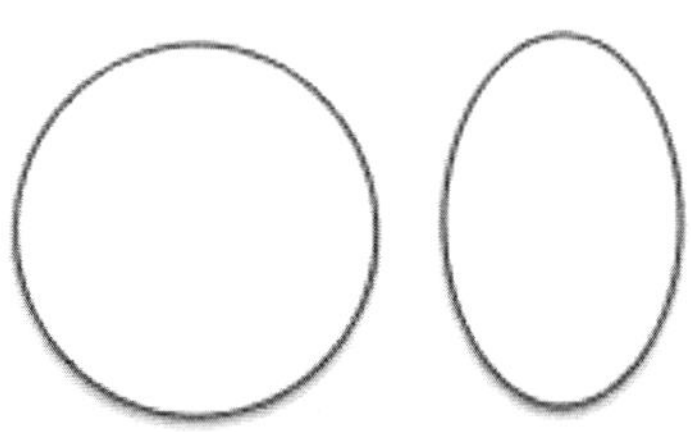

d. 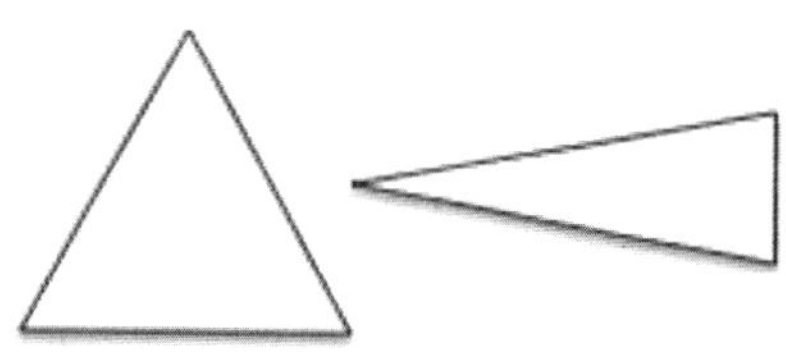

9. A student is attempting to prove that opposite angles of a parallelogram are congruent. In the following section, what should the student write for #5?

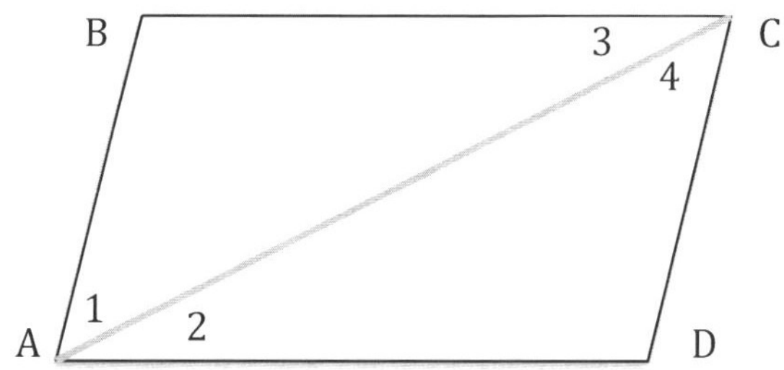

1.	$ABCD$ is a parallelogram	1.	Given
2.	Draw AC	2.	Two points determine a line.
3.	$AB \parallel DC; AD \parallel BC$	3.	Definition of a parallelogram (a quadrilateral with 2 pairs of sides, opposite sides parallel).
4.	$\angle 1 \cong \angle 4;\ \angle 2 \cong \angle 3$	4.	If 2 parallel lines are cut by a transversal, alternate interior angles are congruent.
5.	$AC \cong AC$	5.	

a. Reflexive Property.
b. Symmetric Property.
c. Transitive Property.
d. CPCTC.

10. If rectangle $ABCD$, pictured below, is dilated by a scale factor of $\frac{3}{2}$ to create its image $A'B'C'D'$, how does the slope of $\overleftrightarrow{AC}$ compare to the slope of $\overleftrightarrow{B'D'}$?

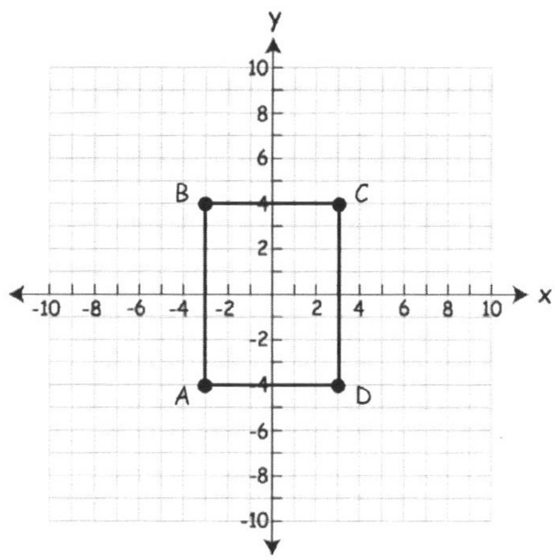

a. The slope of $\overleftrightarrow{B'D'}$ is $\frac{3}{2}$ of the slope of $\overleftrightarrow{AC}$.
b. The slope of $\overleftrightarrow{B'D'}$ is $-\frac{2}{3}$ of the slope of $\overleftrightarrow{AC}$.
c. The slope of $\overleftrightarrow{B'D'}$ is the opposite reciprocal of the slope of $\overleftrightarrow{AC}$.
d. The slope of $\overleftrightarrow{B'D'}$ is the opposite of the slope of $\overleftrightarrow{AC}$.

11. If the two right triangles below are similar, what is the perimeter of triangle *MNP*?

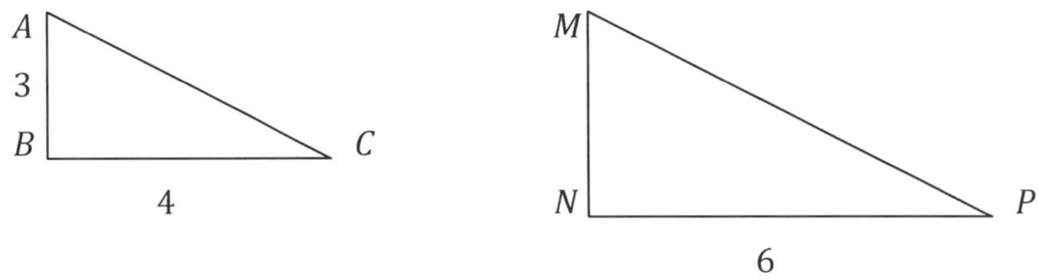

a. 4.5
b. 7.5
c. 12
d. 18

12. In ΔABC, $\cos A =$

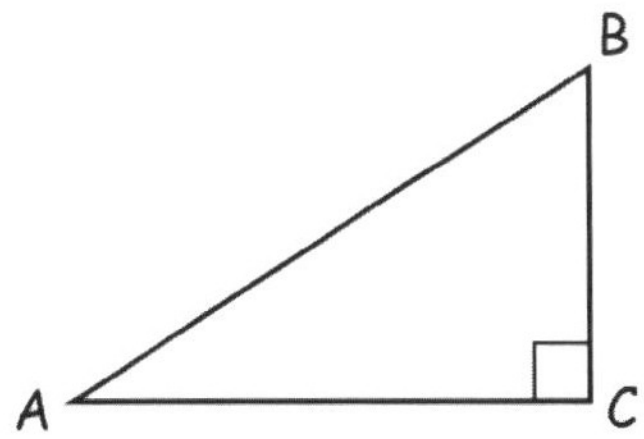

a. $\sin(90 - A)$
b. $\cos(90 - A)$
c. $\tan(90 - \text{A})$
d. $\sec(90 - \text{A})$

13. Right triangle *XYZ* is divided into two smaller right triangles as pictured. If *XY* is 8 and *XZ* is 15, what is the value of *WX*?

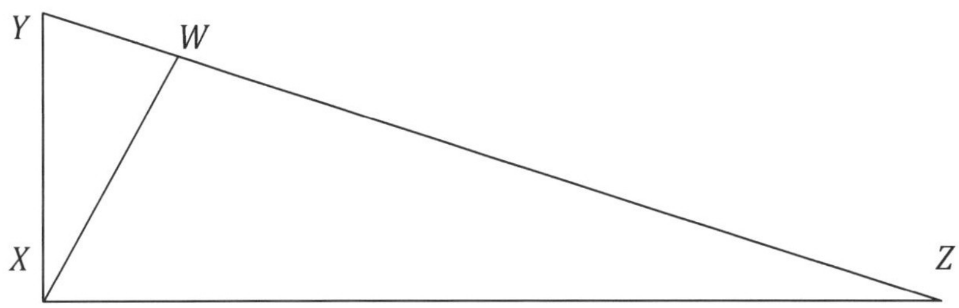

a. $\frac{120}{17}$
b. 17
c. $\frac{225}{17}$
d. $\frac{64}{17}$

14. Based on ΔABC below, what is the value of x?

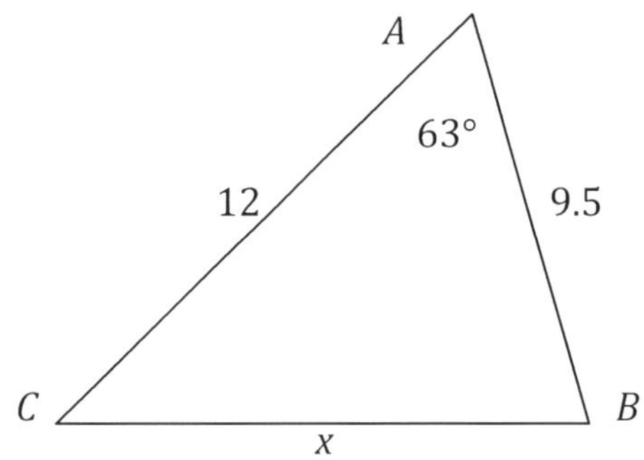

a. 5.6
b. 7.3
c. 11.4
d. 15.3

15. What is the length of the segment connecting the points (–3,2) and (6,–10)?

a. 9
b. 10.5
c. 12
d. 15

16. What are the coordinates of the midpoint of (6, –3) and (0, 7)?

a. (3, 5)
b. (3, 2)
c. (6, 4)
d. (6, 10)

17. A parallelogram is drawn on a coordinate plane. Its vertices are located at (0, 0), (–3, 3), (0, 4), and (x, y). If (x, y) is located in Quadrant I, what are the coordinates of (x, y)?

a. (–3, –1)
b. (2, 1)
c. (3, 1)
d. (3, –1)

18. The vertices of an isosceles triangle are located at (3, 2), (4.5, –7), and (6, 2). What is the area of the triangle?

a. 27
b. 21.25
c. 13.5
d. 9

19. If the diameter of Circle A is 12 cm and the radius of circle B is 15 cm, what is the ratio of the area of Circle A to the area of Circle B?

a. $\frac{4}{25}$
b. $\frac{16}{25}$
c. $\frac{2}{5}$
d. $\frac{4}{5}$

20. If a quadrilateral is inscribed in a circle, opposite angles are _______________.

a. acute
b. equal
c. complementary
d. supplementary

21. In Circle *P* below, what is the area of sector *NPQ*?

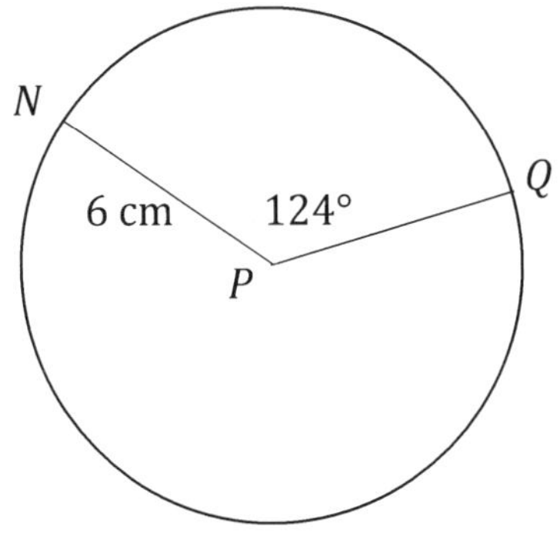

a. 13.0 cm^2
b. 38.9 cm^2
c. 113.0 cm^2
d. 155.7 cm^2

22. What is the center of the circle described by the equation $(x-3)^2+(y+6)^2-16=0$?

a. $(-3,6)$
b. $(3,-6)$
c. $(-6,12)$
d. $(9,36)$

23. What is the diameter of the circle described by the equation $x^2-x+y^2-6y=-\frac{33}{4}$?

a. $\frac{33}{2}$
b. $\sqrt{33}$
c. 1
d. 2

24. A shipping container in the shape of a rectangular prism measures 610 cm by 315 cm by 370 cm. What is the surface area?

a. $1.30x10^3$ cm^2
b. $5.34x10^5$ cm^2
c. $1.07x10^6$ cm^2
d. $7.11x10^7$ cm^2

25. The image below is the net of a square pyramid. What is the pyramid's volume (figure not drawn to scale)?

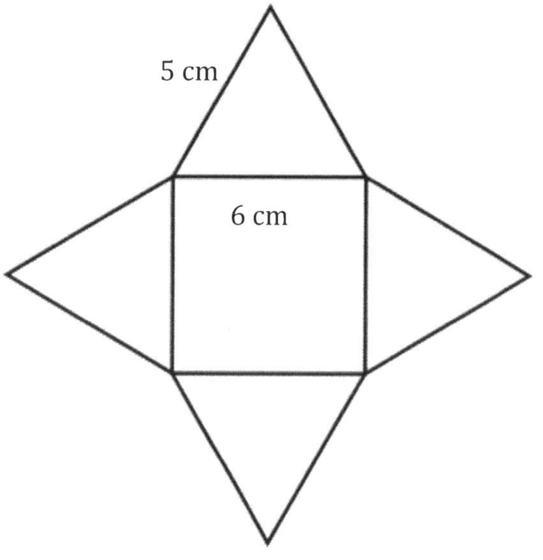

a. 36 cm^2
b. 48 cm^3
c. $12\sqrt{7}$ cm^3
d. 84 cm^2

For questions 26–35, select one or more answers from the answer choices.

26. Which of the following pairs of triangles can be proved to be congruent by SAS?

a. 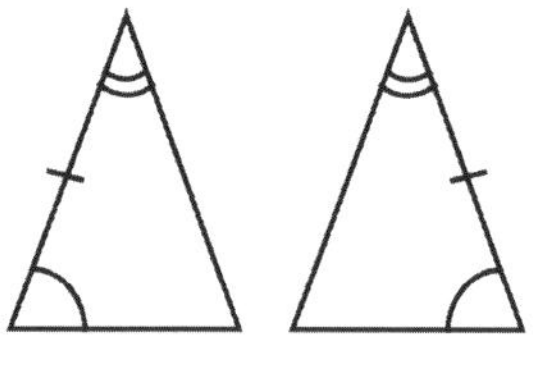

b. 

c. 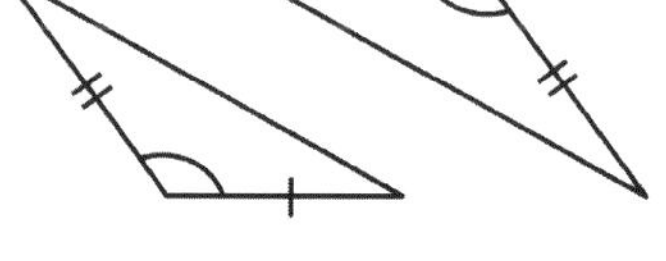

d. 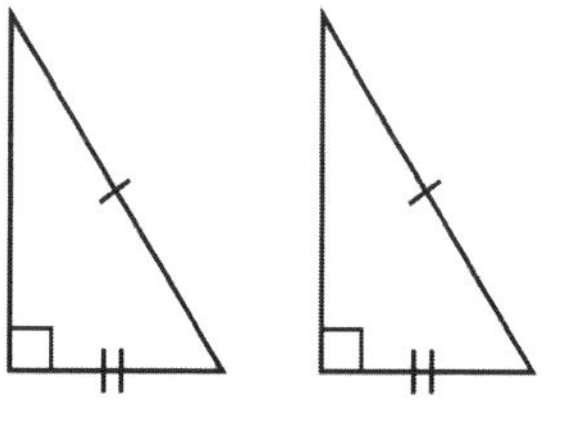

27. The following steps describe the construction of one or more shapes inscribed in a circle. If Step 6 is to connect some or all of the six points, which shapes are possible?

Step 1 – Using a compass, draw a circle.
Step 2 – Keeping the radius of the compass fixed, mark a point on the circle.
Step 3 – Centered at that point, draw an arc across the circle and mark a point at that intersection.
Step 4 – Center the compass at that new point, draw another arc across the circle and mark that point.
Step 5 – Continue drawing arcs along the circle until there are six points.

a. Equilateral Triangle
b. Regular Hexagon
c. Regular Pentagon
d. Square

28. In right triangles *ABC* and *DEF* below, angles *A* and *D* both measure 71°. Which of the following theorems can be used to prove that $\Delta ABC \sim \Delta DEF$ (figures not drawn to scale)?

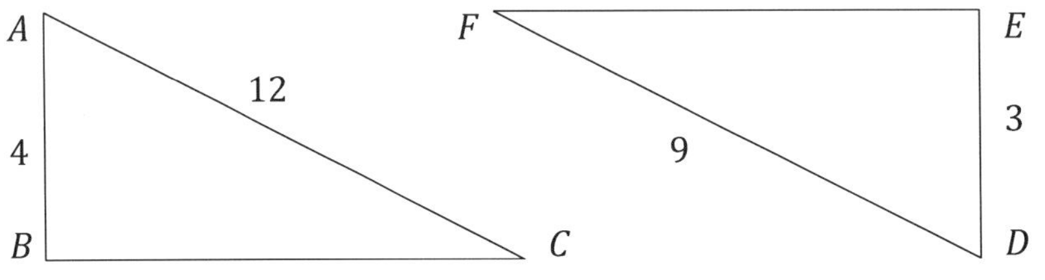

a. AA
b. SSS
c. SAS
d. AAA

29. Cos 47° is equivalent to which of the following values?

a. sin 137°
b. sin 223°
c. cos 227°
d. cos 313°

30. Quadrilateral *ABCD* has vertices at (-2,3), (0,4), (1,1), and (-1,0). What shape is it?

a. Square
b. Rectangle
c. Parallelogram
d. Rhombus

31. A volleyball has a radius of 4*r* inches. What is the ball's circumference?

a. $4\pi r$ in
b. $8\pi r$ in
c. $\frac{2\pi r}{3}$ ft
d. $\frac{4\pi r^3}{81}$ ft

32. A circle has a center at (0, -2) and passes through the point (-3, -2). Which of the following points also lie on the circle?

a. $(0, -5)$
b. $(-2, 0)$
c. $(0, 1)$
d. $\left(\frac{3\sqrt{3}}{2}, -\frac{1}{2}\right)$

33. A circle has a radius of 6 and a center at (-2, 4). Which of the following equations describes that circle?

a. $(x-2)^2 + (y+4)^2 = 36$
b. $x^2 + 4x + y^2 - 8y = 16$
c. $x^2 + 12 + y^2 + 4x - 8y - 8 = 20$
d. $(x+2)^2 - 4 + (y-4)^2 + 9 = 41$

34. A cylindrical storage tank has a diameter of 6 m and a height of 18 m. How much will the tank hold?

a. $5.087x10^8$ cm³
b. $2.035x10^{12}$ mm³
c. $5.087x10^{-7}$ km³
d. 2035 m³

35. Which of the following are possible two-dimensional shapes that can be formed from the various cross-sections of a cone?

a. Circle
b. Ellipse
c. Trapezoid
d. Parabola

For questions 36–50, enter a numerical answer.

36. In triangle *XYZ* below, a perpendicular bisector of side *XZ* is drawn, creating segment *WY*. If *XY* = 3x + 1, *WX* = 4x – 6, and *WZ* = 3x – 3, what is the length of *YZ*?

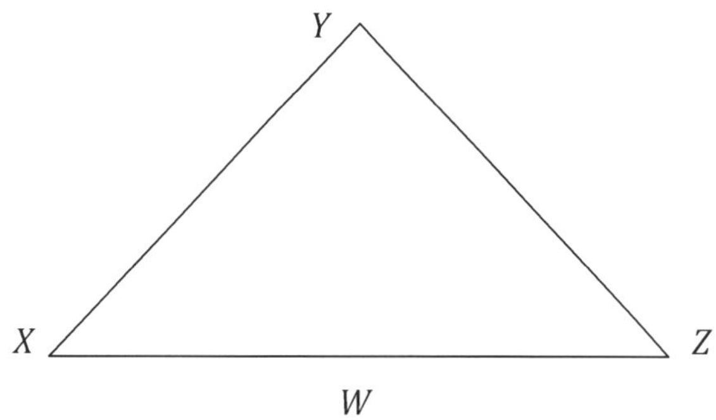

37. **A rectangle is attached to a right triangle as shown below. What is the perimeter of the figure?**

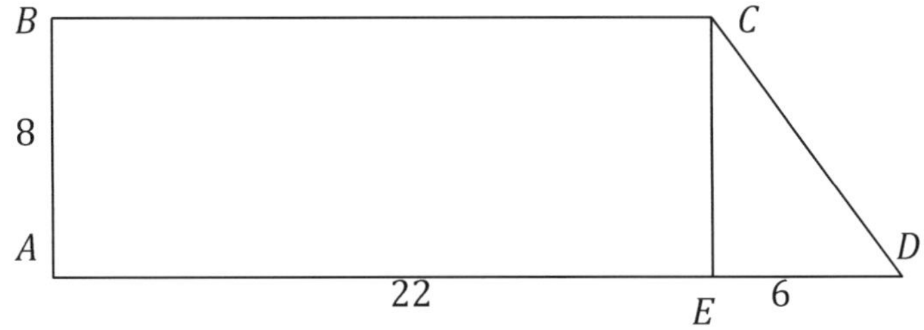

38. **Triangles *MNP* and *QRS* below are congruent. If *MP* is 12, *NP* is 3*x*+7, *QR* is 5, and *RS* is 12*x* – 2, what is the perimeter of triangle *QRS*?**

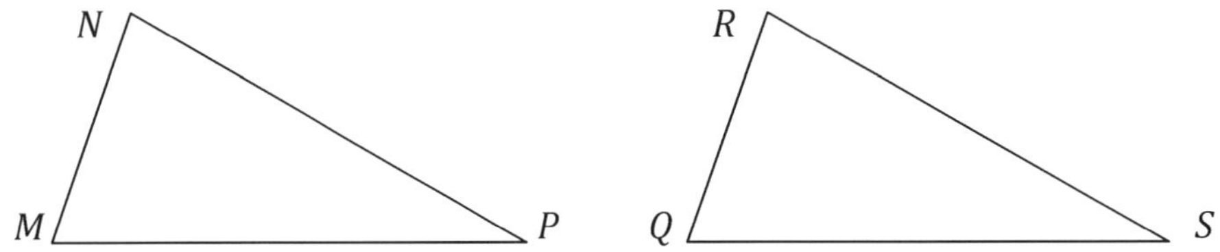

39. **If triangle *DEF* below is dilated by a factor of $\frac{1}{2}$ to become triangle *HJK*, what is the measure of angle *H*?**

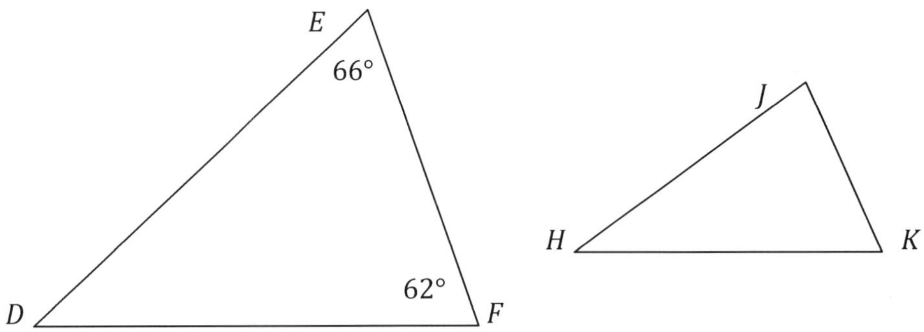

40. A wire is attached to a telephone pole at a point 38 feet above the ground and is staked in the ground a distance from the pole as seen in the figure below. What is the measure of the angle between the ground and the wire (x)? Round to the nearest whole degree.

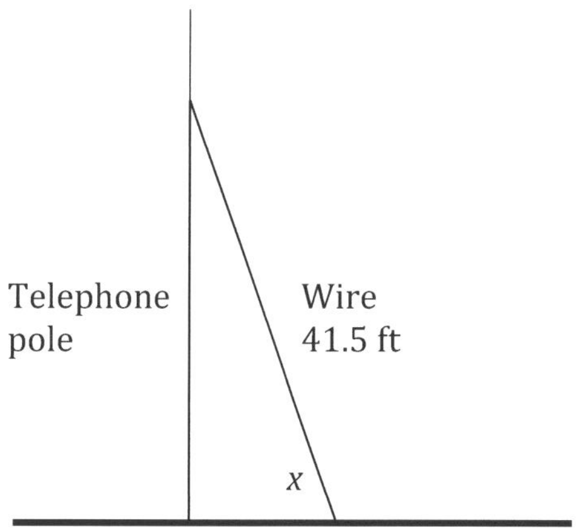

41. Jordan and Liz both live within walking distance of a skateboard park, as seen in the graphic below. How far apart are their homes, rounded to the nearest foot?

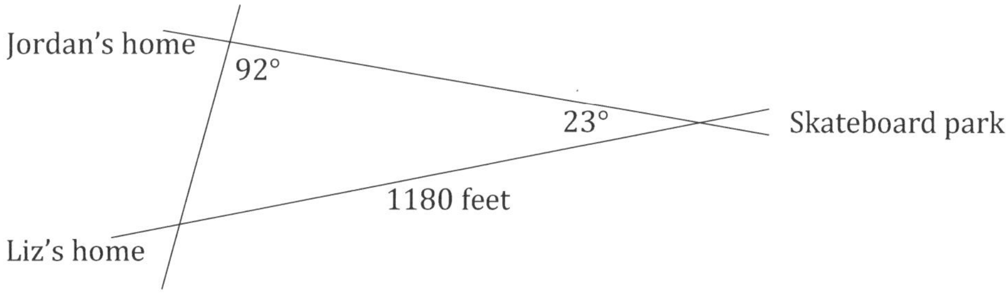

42. **Marc and Aliyah stood next to each other. Then Marc walked 16 feet west and 12 feet north, while Aliyah walked 10 feet east and 24 feet south. How far apart are they?**

43. **Find the perimeter of the parallelogram defined by the points (−3, 0), (0, 4), (8, 4), and (5, 0).**

44. **Find the central angle of a circle if the arc length is 5 inches and the radius is 8 inches (round to the nearest whole degree).**

45. **In Circle *O* below, segment *MN* is tangent to the circle. If the radius of the circle is 12, what is the length of *NO*?**

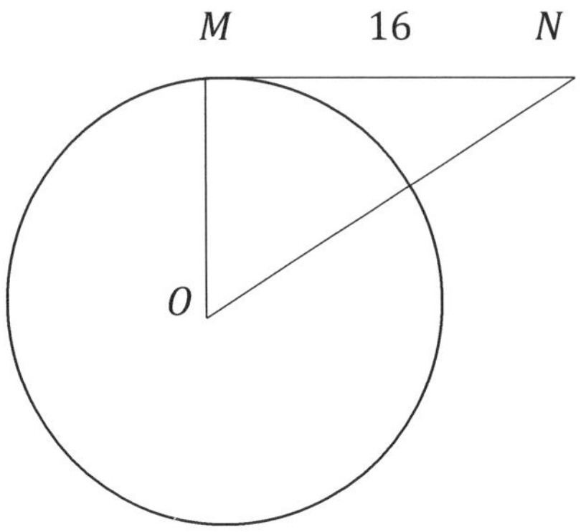

46. **Quadrilateral *MNPQ* is inscribed in a circle as seen below. What is the measure of ∠*PQM*?**

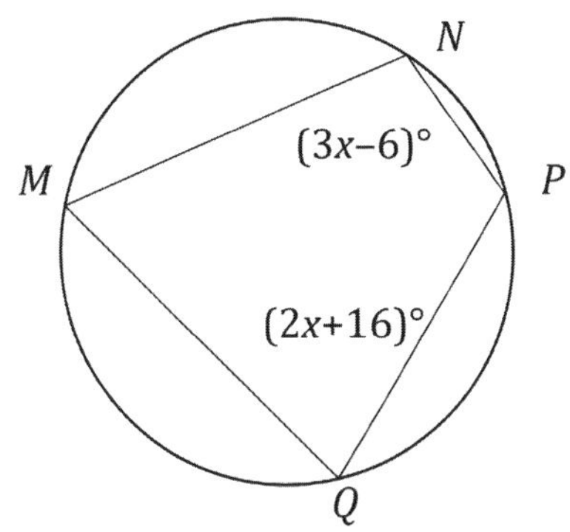

47. The sides of quadrilateral *ABCD* are tangent to the circle. What is the perimeter of *ABCD*?

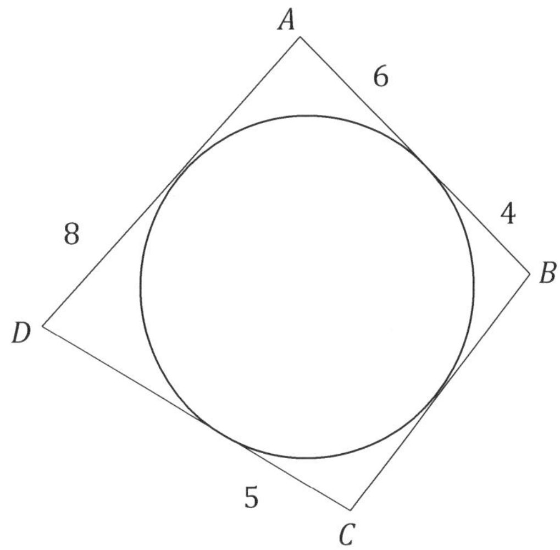

48. What is the area of sector *AOB* in Circle *O* below, rounded to the nearest square centimeter?

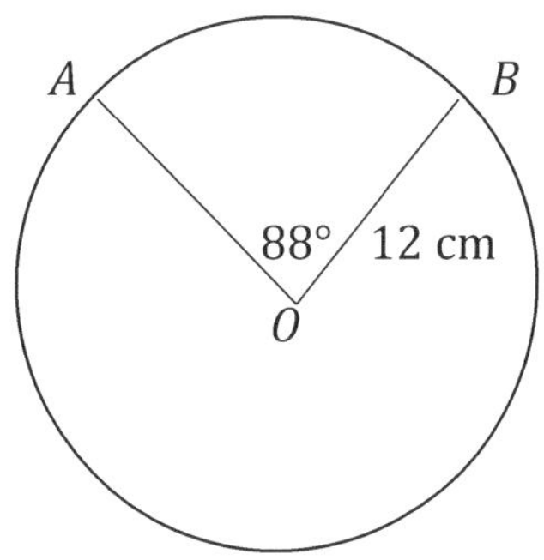

49. The radius of a sphere is 4 inches. If the radius is increased to 12, the volume of the sphere will increase by what factor?

50. Jana is building a rectangular raised garden bed. She purchases soil to fill it for $4.50 per bag, and each bag contains 1.5 cubic feet of soil. If the dimensions of the garden bed are 8 ft × 6 ft × 1.5 ft, how much will Jana pay to completely fill it with soil (answer in whole dollars)?

Answer Key and Explanations for Test #1

1. C: According to the Triangle Sum Theorem, the measures of the three angles in a triangle sum to 180°. Therefore, in the triangle shown, $m\angle X + m\angle Y + m\angle Z = 180°$. However, we are not initially given the measure of ∠X. But, since the triangle is isosceles, the Isosceles Triangle Theorem states that in an isosceles triangle, the base angles (or angles opposite the congruent sides) are congruent. So, in this triangle, $m\angle X = m\angle Z$. By substitution, the angle measure equation becomes $4x - 12 + 32 + 4x - 12 = 180$. Simplifying the left side of the equation becomes $8x + 8 = 180$. After subtracting 8 from both sides, the equation becomes $8x = 172$. Finally, divide both sides by 8 to get $x = 21.5$. Then, substitute that value for x into the expression for the measure of ∠X: $4(21.5) - 12 = 86 - 12 = 74°$. Answer A incorrectly assumed that the ∠X and ∠Y were the congruent angles in the isosceles triangle. Answer B incorrectly doubled the measure of ∠Y. Answer D incorrectly set up the equation as $4x - 12 + 32 = 180$ to get the angle measure of 148°.

2. B: In ΔABC, the midpoints are marked as D, E, and F. The medians of the triangle are then drawn in as $\overline{AF}$, $\overline{BD}$ and $\overline{CE}$. The medians intersect at a point called the centroid, G. Based on this intersection, it is the case that $AG = 2GF$, $BG = 2GD$, and $CG = 2GE$. Thus $CG = \frac{2}{3}CE$. Since we are given that $CE = 6x - 9$ and $CG = 2x + 3$, we can set up the equation as $2x + 3 = \frac{2}{3}(6x - 9)$. Simplifying that equation, it becomes $2x + 3 = 4x - 6$. After subtracting $4x$ and 3 from both sides, the equation becomes $-2x = -9$, or $x = 4.5$. Then, we can calculate the length of CE: $6(4.5) - 9 = 18$. The length of CG is: $2(4.5) + 3 = 12$. So $GE = CE - CG = 18 - 12 = 6$. Answer A is the value of x. Answer C is the length of CG. Answer D is the length of CE.

3. C: One of the theorems about parallelograms states that the opposite angles in a parallelogram are congruent. Therefore, according to the figure, $\angle BAD \cong \angle DCB$, so $m\angle BAD = m\angle DCB$. By substitution, that equation becomes $2x - 13 = 3x - 58$. After subtracting $3x$ from both sides and adding 13 to both sides, the equation simplifies as $-x = -45$, or $x = 45$. To find the measure of ∠DCB, we first substitute the value for x into the expression for ∠DCB: $3(45) - 58 = 135 - 58 = 77°$. Answer A is the measure of ∠DCB if the angles were incorrectly thought to be complementary angles. Answer B is just the value of x. Answer D is the measure of ∠DCB is the angles were incorrectly thought to be supplementary angles.

4. A: Perpendicular lines are two distinct lines in the same plane that intersect at a right angle. Answer B is the definition of parallel lines. Answer C is the definition of opposite rays, which form a line. Answer D is the definition of an angle.

5. D: The slope of the original line is $m = -\frac{3}{4}$. Since the new line needs to be perpendicular, the new slope needs to be the negative reciprocal of the original slope. The negative reciprocal of $-\frac{3}{4}$ is $\frac{4}{3}$. The given point is (0, 6), which is equivalent to (x_1, y_1) in the point-slope equation of $y - y_1 = m(x - x_1)$. Substituting in the new slope and given point, the point-slope equation becomes $y - 6 = \frac{4}{3}(x - 0)$. Distributing on the right side of the equation results in $y - 6 = \frac{4}{3}x$. Add 6 to both sides of the equation to get the perpendicular line of $y = \frac{4}{3}x + 6$. Answer A took the opposite slope instead of the opposite reciprocal slope. Answer B found a parallel line. Answer C took the reciprocal slope instead of the opposite reciprocal slope.

6. C: The listed angles are located in the alternate interior angles position. According to the Alternate Interior Angle Theorem, when a transversal cuts across parallel lines, the alternate interior angles are congruent. Since lines a and b are parallel, it means that $4x - 18 = 3x + 21$. After subtracting $3x$ from both sides and adding 18 to both sides, the equation simplifies as $x = 39$. In Answer A, the angles were incorrectly treated as complementary. In Answer B, the angles were incorrectly treated as supplementary. Answer D is the measure of each alternate interior angle, but the question only wanted the value of x.

7. C: A 270° clockwise rotation is the same as a 90° counterclockwise rotation about the origin. The values of x and y are switched and the x-value becomes negative. Answer A is the coordinate change for a 180° rotation (either clockwise or counterclockwise). Answer B is the coordinate change after a 90° clockwise rotation about the origin. Answer D is the coordinate change after a reflection across the line $y = x$.

8. B: In order for two figures to be congruent, they must have the same size and shape. The two triangles in Answer A are not the same size and shape, as the second triangle is larger. The parallelograms in Answer B are the same size and shape, even though one is rotated. In Answer C, the second circle has been vertically stretched, so the figures are not the same shape or size. In Answer D, the second triangle has a much smaller base than the first.

9. A: The property that a segment or angle is congruent to itself is termed the reflexive property. The other three choices all deal with comparing two different areas to each other.

10. D: Since rectangle $ABCD$ is centered at the origin and $\overleftrightarrow{AC}$ passes through the origin, any dilation of rectangle $ABCD$ will leave the slopes of the diagonals unchanged. Since A has the coordinates (−3, −4) and C has the coordinates (3, 4), the slope of $\overleftrightarrow{AC} = \frac{4-(-4)}{3-(-3)} = \frac{8}{6} = \frac{4}{3}$. When rectangle $ABCD$ is dilated by a scale factor of $\frac{3}{2}$ to create image $A'B'C'D'$, B' has the coordinates $\left(-\frac{9}{2}, 6\right)$ and D' has the coordinates $\left(\frac{9}{2}, -6\right)$. The slope of $\overleftrightarrow{B'D'} = \frac{6-(-6)}{-4.5-4.5} = \frac{12}{-9} = -\frac{4}{3}$. Therefore, the slope of $\overleftrightarrow{B'D'}$ is the opposite of the slope of $\overleftrightarrow{AC}$. The scale factor does not affect the slope, so answers A and B are incorrect. Answer C refers to a perpendicular line, but since $ABCD$ is not a square, the diagonals are not perpendicular.

11. D: Since we know that the two triangles are similar, we know that the ratio of each side to its corresponding side in the other triangle is the same. So, we can solve for side MN by setting up a ratio: $\frac{4}{6} = \frac{3}{MN}$. Then we cross-multiply: $4MN = 3(6)$, or $MN = \frac{3(6)}{4} = 4.5$. Then we can solve for the hypotenuse, MP, by using the **Pythagorean theorem**: $4.5^2 + 6^2 = MP^2$, or $56.25 = MP^2$. We take the square root of each side to find that MP is 7.5. Finally, we add the three sides of triangle MNP to find that the perimeter is $4.5 + 6 + 7.5 = 18$. Answer A is the length of side MN. Answer B is the length of side MP. Answer C is the perimeter of triangle ABC.

12. A: The cosine function is represented by the ratio $\frac{adjacent\ leg}{hypotenuse}$. In ΔABC, this can be written as $\frac{AC}{AB}$. The sine function is represented by the ratio $\frac{opposite\ leg}{hypotenuse}$. So, the sine of angle B can also be written as $\frac{AC}{AB}$. Since this is a right triangle, angles A and B are complementary; that is, they add up to 90°. So, angle B can be written as $90° - A$. Thus $\cos A = \sin(90 - A)$. Answer B gives the cosine of angle B, or $\frac{BC}{AB}$. Answer C gives the tangent of angle B, which is represented by the ratio $\frac{opposite\ leg}{adjacent\ leg}$, or $\frac{AC}{BC}$.

Answer D gives the secant of angle B, which is the reciprocal of the cosine and is represented by the ratio $\frac{hypotenuse}{adjacent\ leg}$, or $\frac{AB}{BC}$.

13. A: Noticing that ΔWYX and ΔWXZ are both complimentary to ΔXYZ, we have that $m\angle WXY = m\angle WZX = m\angle XZY$. By Angle Angle similarity, we know these are similar triangles. By the **Pythagorean theorem**, $YZ = \sqrt{XY^2 + XZ^2} = \sqrt{8^2 + 15^2} = 17$. Because WYX is similar to WXZ, we have the ratio $\frac{WX}{XY} = \frac{XZ}{YZ}$. Solving for WX yields $WX = \frac{XY \cdot XZ}{YZ} = \frac{8 \cdot 15}{17} = \frac{120}{17}$. Answer B is the length of YZ. Answer C is the length of WZ. Answer D is the length of WY.

14. C: In the figure, since the given angle is located between the two given sides, we need to use the Law of Cosines to solve for x. The Law of Cosines is $c^2 = a^2 + b^2 - 2ab\cos(C)$. If we let $a = 12$, $b = 9.5$ and $c = x$, then the Law of Cosines becomes $x^2 = 12^2 + 9.5^2 - 2(12)(9.5)\cos(63°)$. This simplifies to $x^2 = 130.74$. Therefore, $x = 11.4$. Answer A used sine instead of cosine in the formula. Answer B incorrectly used the **Pythagorean theorem** with $x^2 + 9.5^2 = 12^2$, instead of using the Law of Cosines. Answer D also incorrectly used the **Pythagorean theorem** with $12^2 + 9.5^2 = x^2$.

15. D: To calculate distance between points, the distance formula can be used: $d = \sqrt{(x_1 - x_2)^2 + (y_1 - y_2)^2}$. We can use the points $(-3,2)$ and $(6,-10)$ for the x- and y-values: $\sqrt{(-3-6)^2 + (2--10)^2} = \sqrt{(-9)^2 + 12^2} = \sqrt{81 + 144} = \sqrt{225} = 15$. Answer A is the difference in the x-values. Answer B is the average of the differences in the x- and y-values. Answer C is the difference in the y-values.

16. B: The midpoint between two points is simply the average of the x-values and the y-values. So, we can calculate the midpoint of (6, –3) and (0, 7): $\left(\frac{6+0}{2}, \frac{-3+7}{2}\right) = (3,2)$. Answer A used 3 instead of –3 for one of the y-coordinates. Answer choice C added the points but did not divide by 2. Answer choice D added the points and used 3 instead of –3 for one of the y-coordinates.

17. C: We can plot the three points on a coordinate plane and call point (0,0) A, point (–3,3) B, point (0,4) C, and point (x, y) D, which is in Quadrant I. Because it is a parallelogram, opposite sides must be parallel, so we can say that side BC is parallel to side AD. Thus, these two segments will have the same slope. The slope of segment BC can be found from the points: $\frac{4-3}{0--3} = \frac{1}{3}$, as moving from point B to point C requires moving up 1 and over 3. So, the slope of line AD will also be $\frac{1}{3}$, and moving from point A to point D can also be described as moving up 1 and over 3. As point A is (0,0), we add 3 to the x-coordinate and 1 to the y-coordinate to find that point D is (3,1). Answer A would be the fourth point if it were located in Quadrant III instead of Quadrant I. Answer D moves over 3 and down 1 instead of up, creating a trapezoid.

18. C: We can plot the three points on the coordinate plane and find the height and base to determine the area. From point (3, 2) to point (6, 2) there is a horizontal distance of 3. This is the base of the triangle. From the midpoint of this segment to point (4.5, –7) there is a vertical distance of 9. So, the triangle has a base of 3 and a height of 9. The area of a triangle can be found by the formula $A = \frac{1}{2}bh$, or $\frac{1}{2}(3)(9) = \frac{27}{2} = 13.5$. Answer A is the area without dividing by 2. Answer B is the perimeter of the triangle. Answer D is the height of the triangle.

19. A: The area of each circle can be found by the formula $A = \pi r^2$. The radius of Circle A is half the diameter, or 6 cm, so the area of Circle A is $\pi(6)^2 = 36\pi$. The radius of Circle B is 15 cm, so the area of Circle B is $\pi(15)^2 = 225\pi$. The ratio of Circle A to Circle B is $\frac{36\pi}{225\pi} = \frac{36}{225} = \frac{4}{25}$. Answer B is the ratio of the areas of the two circles if both given measurements are treated as the diameter or as the radius, rather than one of each. Answer C is the ratio of the circumferences of the two circles. Answer D is the ratio of the circumferences of the two circles if both given measurements are treated as the diameter or as the radius, rather than one of each.

20. D: One of the basic circle theorems states that for any quadrilateral inscribed in a circle (cyclic quadrilateral), opposite angles sum to 180°, so they are supplementary. These angles cannot both be acute (answer A) or they will not sum to 180°. The angles may be equal (answer B) if they are both 90°, but are not necessarily equal. The angles cannot be complementary (answer C), summing to 90°, because then the four angles of the quadrilateral would only add up to 180° instead of the 360° of any quadrilateral.

21. B: The area of the sector of a circle is calculated using the equation: $\frac{Central\ Angle\ Measure}{360°} \times \pi r^2$, where r is the radius of the circle. Since the central angle measure is 124° and the radius is 6 cm, the equation becomes: $\frac{124°}{360°} \times \pi(6\ cm)^2$= 38.9 cm^2. Answer A found the length of arc NQ. Answer C is the area of the circle. Answer D used the diameter length instead of the radius in the calculation.

22. B: Since this equation is already in standard form, we can find the center by setting each parenthetical term equal to zero: $x - 3 = 0 \Rightarrow x = 3$, so the x-coordinate of the center is 3. The y-coordinate is: $y + 6 = 0 \Rightarrow y = -6$. So, the center is at $(3, -6)$. Answer A reverses the signs, taking the numbers straight from the equation rather than setting each term equal to zero. Answer C doubles the values directly from the original equation. Answer D squares the values in the original equation.

23. D: We begin by isolating x- and y-terms and completing the square: $x^2 - x + \frac{1}{4} + y^2 - 6y + 9 = -\frac{33}{4} + \frac{1}{4} + 9$. This simplifies to: $\left(x - \frac{1}{2}\right)^2 + (y - 3)^2 = 1$. The radius is the root of the variable on the right side of the equal sign when the equation is in this format, so $r = \sqrt{1} = 1$. The diameter is twice the radius, or 2. Answer A takes the value to the right of the equal sign in the original equation as the radius (ignoring the sign). Answer B takes the value to the right of the equal sign in the original equation as the radius squared (ignoring the sign). Answer C is the radius.

24. C: A rectangular pyramid has six rectangular faces. We can calculate these as follows: $SA = 2bh + 2bw + 2hw$, where b is the base, h is the height, and w is the width. We can let $b = 610$, $h = 315$, and $w = 370$. So $SA = 2(610)(315) + 2(610)(370) + 2(315)(370) = 1{,}068{,}800$. We can write this in scientific notation by moving the decimal six places to the left and rounding: $1.07x10^6$. Answer A adds the three dimensions together rather than calculating area of each side. Answer B does not double each portion of the surface area. Answer D is the volume of the shipping container.

25. C: Each side of the square base is 6 cm, so the area of the base is $B = 36$ cm^2. To find the height, we first must find the height of one of the triangular faces. We can divide a face in half to create a right triangle with a base of 3 (half of 6):

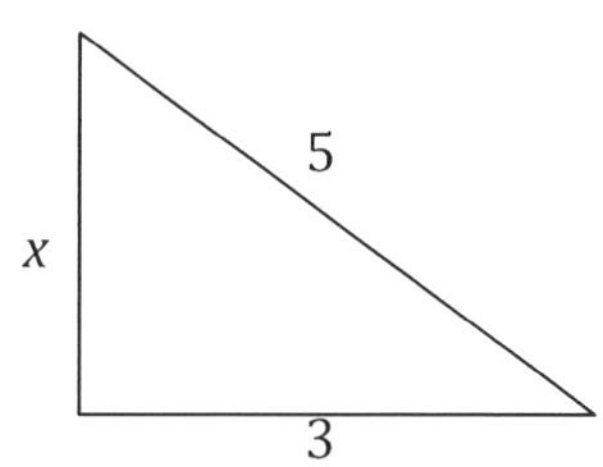

Then we can use the **Pythagorean theorem** to solve for the height of the triangle:

$$a^2 + b^2 = c^2$$
$$x^2 + 3^2 = 5^2$$
$$x^2 + 9 = 25$$
$$x^2 = 16$$
$$x = 4$$

Now we need the height of the actual pyramid, since the triangular faces will be slanted to meet above the square base. The value of x in the triangle above becomes the slant height of the pyramid as seen in the bold line in the pyramid below. Then we can draw a new right triangle using this slant height as the hypotenuse and 3 (half of the side of the square base) as the base to find the height of the pyramid:

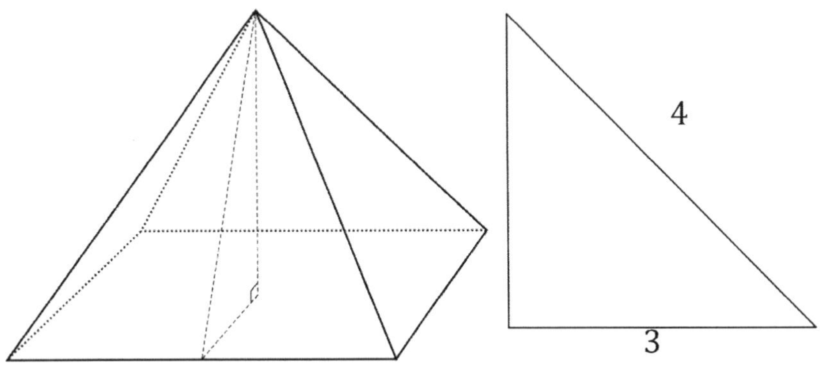

We use the **Pythagorean theorem** again:

$$h^2 + 3^2 = 4^2$$
$$h^2 + 9 = 16$$
$$h^2 = 7$$
$$h = \sqrt{7}$$

Now we can calculate the volume of the pyramid:

$$V = \frac{1}{3}Bh$$
$$V = \frac{1}{3}(36)\sqrt{7}$$
$$V = 12\sqrt{7}\text{ cm}^3$$

Answer A is the area of the base. Answer B is the surface area of the pyramid. Answer D is the volume of the pyramid using the slant height instead of the actual height.

26. B, C: SAS stands for "Side Angle Side," and can be used to prove that two triangles are similar when two sides, along with the angle between the two sides, are similar in both triangles. Answers B and C each have two pairs of congruent sides, along with the angle between these two sides, so they can be proven to be congruent by SAS. Answer A has two triangles that are congruent by ASA (Angle Side Angle). Answer D has two right triangles that are congruent by HL (Hypotenuse Leg).

27. A, B: The listed steps could describe the construction of an equilateral triangle inscribed in a circle if every other point was connected. If every point was connected using a straightedge, that would have constructed a regular hexagon instead. A regular pentagon (C) and square (D) are impossible because with six evenly spaced possible vertices, it is impossible to create a shape with four or five sides of equal length.

28. A, C: We can see that the hypotenuse of triangle *DEF* is $\frac{3}{4}$ of the hypotenuse of triangle *ABC*, and the short leg of triangle *DEF* is likewise $\frac{3}{4}$ of the short leg of triangle *ABC*. Since the proportions are the same, the given angle is the same, and the right angles are the same, we can prove similarity in different ways. On triangle *ABC* we know two sides, side *AC* and side *AB*, and the angle between them. We also know that angle *B* is 90° since we are told that it is a right triangle. For triangle *DEF*, we are given the corresponding information. We can use AA (Angle Angle) because if two angles of the triangles are congruent, the third must be also, since the interior angles of a triangle always add up to 180°. We can use ASA (Angle Side Angle) by using angle *A*, side *AB*, and angle *B*, comparing with angle *D*, side *DE*, and angle *E*. We cannot use SSS (Side Side Side) since we do not know all three sides. Likewise, we cannot use AAA (Angle Angle Angle) as we are only given two angles.

29. A, D: The cosine of one angle is equivalent to the cosine of the complementary angle. Therefore, since 90° – 47° = 43°, then cos 47° = sin 43°. In Answer A, sin 137° is the Quadrant II equivalent to sin 43°; it is 43° above the *y*-axis in this quadrant just as 43° is in Quadrant I, and is still positive. In Answer D, cos 313° is the Quadrant IV equivalent to cos 47° because it is 47° below the *y*-axis and is still positive. Answers B and C would be correct except that sin and cos are both negative in Quadrant III.

30. C: We can plot the four points and draw the quadrilateral, then find the length and slope of each side to see what kind it is. Let point *A* be (–2,3), point *B* be (0,4), point *C* be (1,1) and point *D* be (–1,0). We find the length of each side by using the distance formula. Side *AB* has a length of $\sqrt{(0--2)^2+(4-3)^2}=\sqrt{5}$ and a slope of $\frac{4-3}{0--2}=\frac{1}{2}$. Side *BC* has a length of $\sqrt{(1-0)^2+(1-4)^2}=\sqrt{10}$ and a slope of $\frac{1-4}{1-0}=-3$. Side *CD* has a length of $\sqrt{(-1-1)^2+(0-1)^2}=\sqrt{5}$ and a slope of $\frac{0-1}{-1-1}=\frac{1}{2}$. Side *DA* has a length of $\sqrt{(-1--2)^2+(0-3)^2}=\sqrt{10}$ and a slope of $\frac{3-0}{-2--1}=-3$. Since *AB* and *CD* have the same length and slope, and *BC* and *DA* also have the same length and slope, we have two pairs of parallel sides, meaning it is a parallelogram. The sides are not all the same length, so it cannot be a square (A) or rhombus (D). To determine if it is a rectangle, we need to know if the angles are right angles. If they are, the slopes of adjacent sides will be perpendicular. In other words, the slopes will be opposite reciprocals of each other. The two slopes are –3 and $\frac{1}{2}$, which are not opposite reciprocals (if they had been –3 and $\frac{1}{3}$ or –2 and $\frac{1}{2}$, they would have been). So, the shape is not a rectangle (B).

31. B, C: The formula for circumference of a circle is $C=\pi d$ or $2\pi r$. If the radius is $4r$, then the circumference is $C=2\pi(4r)=8\pi r$ inches. This can be converted to feet by dividing by 12: $C=\frac{8\pi r}{12}=\frac{2\pi r}{3}$ feet. Answer A treats the radius as the diameter. Answer D finds the volume of the volleyball in feet.

32. A, C, D: A circle centered at (0, –2) that passes through the point (–3, –2) has a radius, *r*, of 3 units, since $r=\sqrt{(0--3)^2+(-2--2)^2}=\sqrt{(3)^2+(0)^2}=\sqrt{9+0}=\sqrt{9}=3.$ The equation for a circle with a center of (0, –2) and *r* = 3 is $(x-0)^2+(y--2)^2=3^2$, which simplifies as

$x^2 + (y + 2)^2 = 9$. We try out the answer choices one by one to see if they work, substituting the points from the answer choices into the circle equation:

Answer A: $0^2 + (-5 + 2)^2 = (-3)^2 = 9$.

Answer B: $(-2)^2 + (0 + 2)^2 = (-2)^2 + 2^2 = 4 + 4 = 8$.

Answer C: $0^2 + (1 + 2)^2 = 3^2 = 9$.

Answer D: $\left(\frac{3\sqrt{3}}{2}\right)^2 + \left(-\frac{1}{2} + 2\right)^2 = \left(\frac{3\sqrt{3}}{2}\right)^2 + \left(\frac{3}{2}\right)^2 = \frac{27}{4} + \frac{9}{4} = \frac{36}{4} = 9$.

Answers A, C, and D all fit the equation, so these are all points on the circle.

33. B, C, D: The equation for a circle is $(x - h)^2 + (y - k)^2 = r^2$, where (h, k) is the center of the circle and r is the radius. Since the center of the circle is (–2, 4) and the radius is 6, those values can be substituted into the equation as $(x - (-2))^2 + (y - 4)^2 = 6^2$ which simplifies as $(x + 2)^2 + (y - 4)^2 = 36$. We can also expand it to $x^2 + 4x + 4 + y^2 - 8y + 16 = 36$, or $x^2 + 4x + y^2 - 8y = 16$. We then check the answers to see which one(s) match these:

Answer A reverses the signs in the parentheses, so it is not a match.

Answer B matches the expanded form above.

Answer C has two constants on the left side of the equation, 12 and –8. When these are subtracted from the 20 on the right, it matches the expanded form above.

Answer D has two constants of the left side of the equation, –4 and 9. When these are subtracted from the 41 on the right, it matches the simplified form above.

34. A, C: The formula for the volume of a cylinder is $V = \pi r^2 h$, where r is the radius and h is the height. Since the cylinder has a diameter of 6 m, the radius is half of the diameter, or 3 m. The height is 18 m. Therefore, by substitution, $V = \pi r^2 h$ becomes $V = \pi(3\ m)^2(18\ m)$= 508.7 m³. This can be converted to other units. To convert to centimeters (Answer A), multiply by 100^3 to obtain $5.087x10^8$ cm³. To convert to millimeters (Answer B), multiply by $1{,}000^3$ to obtain $5.087x10^{11}$ mm³. To convert to kilometers, divide by $1{,}000^3$ to obtain $5.087x10^{-7}$ km³. Answers B and D used the diameter instead of the radius.

35. A, B, and D: When a cross-section is taken of a cone, it can form a circle if the cross-section is parallel to the base of the cone. If taken at an angle across the cone, it can form an ellipse. If taken through the side and base of the cone, it can form a parabola. A trapezoid with four straight edges is impossible.

36. The correct answer is 10: Since segment *WY* bisects side *XZ*, we know that *WX* and *WZ* are equal, so we can set them equal to each other: $4x - 6 = 3x - 3$. Subtracting $3x$ from each side and adding 6 to each side yields $x = 3$. The Perpendicular Bisector Theorem states that the points on a perpendicular bisector of a line segment are exactly those equidistant from the segment's endpoints. Since the point Y lies on *WY*, the perpendicular bisector of *XZ*, it means that the point *Y* is equidistant from both *X* and *Z*, giving us *XY* = *YZ*. Therefore, *YZ* = *XY* = $3x + 1 = 3(3) + 1 = 10$.

I.PGPSCPC.C.1

37. The correct answer is 68: To find the perimeter of the figure, we need to find the length of the two unknown sides. Since figure *ABCE* is a rectangle, we know that side *BC* is equivalent to side *AE*, or 22. To find the length of *CD*, we can use the **Pythagorean theorem**. We know that side *CE* is 8, so $CD^2 = 6^2 + 8^2 = 36 + 64 = 100$, so $CD = \sqrt{100} = 10$. Thus, the perimeter can be calculated: $AB + BC + CD + DE + EA = 8 + 22 + 10 + 6 + 22 = 68$.

38. The correct answer is 27: In order to find the perimeter of ΔQRS, we need to know the values of all three sides of the triangle. We are given that $QR = 5$. Since $\Delta MNP \cong \Delta QRS$, then $QS = MP$, which means that $QS = 12$. Also, since $\Delta MNP \cong \Delta QRS$, then $RS = NP$. Therefore, $12x - 2 = 3x + 7$. After subtracting $3x$ from both sides and adding 2 to both sides, the equation becomes $9x = 9$. Divide both sides by 9 to get $x = 1$. After substituting for *x*, the value of *RS* becomes $12(1) - 2 = 10$. The perimeter of ΔQRS then becomes $5 + 10 + 12 = 27$.

39. The correct answer is 52: Dilation changes the length of the legs of a triangle, but not the angles, as proportions remain the same. So, angle *H* is equal to angle *D*. We can solve for angle *D* by adding angles *E* and *F* and subtracting from 180°: $180 - (66 + 62) = 180 - 128 = 52°$.

40. The correct answer is 66: The telephone pole, the wire, and the ground form a right triangle. The wire forms the hypotenuse and the telephone pole forms the leg opposite of angle *x*. Therefore, in order to solve for the measure of angle *x*, it needs to be set up as $\sin x = \frac{opposite\ leg}{hypotenuse}$ or $\sin x = \frac{38}{41.5}$. The value of *x* is found using the calculation $x = \sin^{-1}\left(\frac{38}{41.5}\right) = 66.3°$, which rounds to 66°.

41. The correct answer is 461: Since the map shows a triangle with a 92° angle, the length of the side opposite the 92° angle, a 23° angle, and it asks for length of the side opposite of the 23° angle (which we will call *x*), the Law of Sines can be used to find the missing side length. The Law of Sines is $\frac{\sin A}{a} = \frac{\sin B}{b} = \frac{\sin C}{c}$, but to solve this problem we only need $\frac{\sin A}{a} = \frac{\sin B}{b}$. By substitution, that equation becomes $\frac{\sin 92°}{1180} = \frac{\sin 23°}{x}$. Solving for *x*, the equation results in $x = \frac{1180 \sin 23°}{\sin 92°} = 461.3$ feet. Rounded to the nearest foot, this is 461 feet.

42. The correct answer is 44.4: The path walked by each person makes a right triangle as seen in the diagram below:

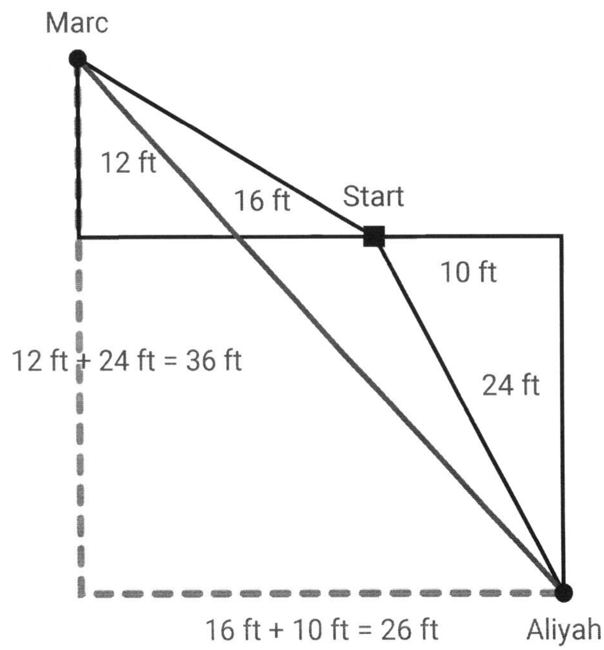

We can calculate the total distance between them by using the Pythagorean theorem:

Total distance $= \sqrt{36^2 + 26^2} = \sqrt{1{,}296 + 676} \approx 44.4$.

So, their total distance apart is about 44.4 feet.

43. The correct answer is 26: We first plot the points to visualize the parallelogram. We can see that two of the sides are horizontal and can use the difference in x-values to find the length. We subtract the x-values for two points that have identical y-values. For example, we can take the points (0, 4) and (8, 4) and subtract 0 from 8 to find that the parallelogram has a length of 8. For the height, we subtract the y-values for two points with differing y-values. For example, we can take the points (−3, 0) and (0, 4) and subtract 0 from 4 to find that the parallelogram has a height of 4. We can then divide the parallelogram into a rectangle and two triangles as seen below to find the length of the diagonal sides:

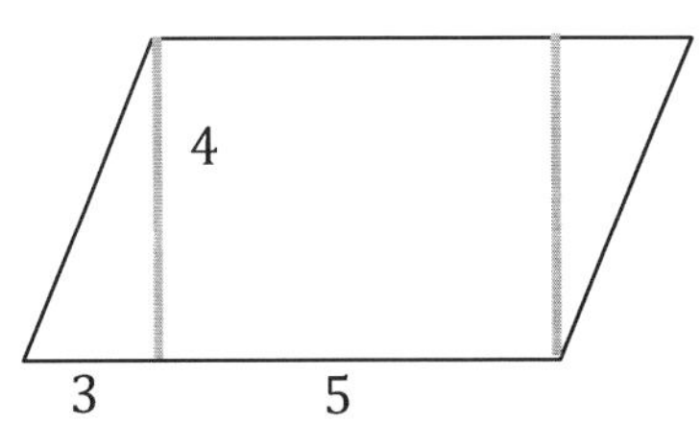

Based on the points, we know that each triangle has a base of 3 and a height of 4. We can then use the **Pythagorean theorem** to find the hypotenuse, or the diagonal side of the parallelogram: $x =$

$\sqrt{3^2 + 4^2} = \sqrt{9 + 16} = \sqrt{25} = 5$. So, the parallelogram has two sides that are 8 and two sides that are 5. We can use the formula for perimeter of a parallelogram: $P = 2l + 2w = 2(8) + 2(5) = 16 + 10 = 26$.

44. The correct answer is 36: The central angle of a circle can be found by setting up a proportion: $\frac{arc\ length}{circumference} = \frac{central\ angle}{360°}$. We can find the circumference: $C = 2\pi r = 2\pi(8) = 16\pi$. Then we let θ be the central angle and set up the proportion: $\frac{5}{16\pi} = \frac{\theta}{360}$. Finally, we cross-multiply and divide: $16\pi\theta = 5(360)$, or $\theta = \frac{5(360)}{16\pi} = \frac{112.5}{\pi} = 35.83°$. Rounded to the nearest whole degree, this is 36°.

45. The correct answer is 20: Since $\overline{MN}$ is tangent to Circle O, $\overline{MN}$ forms a right angle with radius $\overline{MO}$. ΔMNO is then a right triangle, so the **Pythagorean theorem** can be used to find the measure of $\overline{NO}$. Therefore, $(NO)^2 = 12^2 + 16^2 = 144 + 256 = 400$. Finally, we take the square root of both sides to find that $NO = 20$.

46. The correct answer is 84: If a quadrilateral is inscribed in a circle, then its opposite angles are supplementary. Therefore, $m\angle MNP + m\angle PQM = 180°$. By substitution, that equation becomes $3x - 6 + 2x + 16 = 180$. The equation simplifies to $5x + 10 = 180$. After subtracting 10 from both sides, the equation becomes $5x = 170$. Divide both sides by 5 to get $x = 34$. Substituting for x in the expression results in $2(34) + 16 = 84°$.

47. The correct answer is 46: For any point outside a circle, there are exactly two lines tangent to the circle passing through that point. Further, the lengths of these line segments from the point to the circle are equal. In this problem, the two segments extending from A both have a length of 6. The two segments extending from B have a length of 4. The two segments extending from C have a length of 5. The two segments extending from D have a length of 8. Therefore, the perimeter of quadrilateral $ABCD$ can be calculated at $6 + 6 + 4 + 4 + 5 + 5 + 8 + 8 = 46$.

48. The correct answer is 111: The central angle is $\frac{88}{360}$ of the whole circle, and so the area of the sector is also $\frac{88}{360}$ of the whole circle. We can find the area of the circle: $A = \pi r^2 = \pi(12)^2 = 144\pi$. Then we multiply by $\frac{88}{360}$ to find the sector's area: $\frac{88}{360} \cdot 144\pi = 35.2\pi \approx 110.53\text{ cm}^2$. Rounded to the nearest centimeter, this is 111 cm^2.

49. The correct answer is 27: We can calculate the volume of the original sphere: $V = \frac{4}{3}\pi r^3 = \frac{4}{3}\pi(4)^3 = \frac{256}{3}\pi\text{ in}^3$. The volume of the new sphere is: $V = \frac{4}{3}\pi r^3 = \frac{4}{3}\pi(12)^3 = 2{,}304\pi\text{ in}^3$. Dividing these, we find: $2{,}304\pi \div \frac{256}{3}\pi = 2{,}304\pi \cdot \frac{3}{256\pi} = \frac{2{,}304(3)}{256} = 27$. So, the volume of the sphere increased by a factor of 27. Alternatively, we can see that the radius increases by a factor of 3 as it changes from 4 to 12. Since we are calculating volume, a cubic measurement, we can take 3 to the third power to find the factor: $3^3 = 27$.

50. The correct answer is 216: The cost for filling the garden bed with soil is calculated by multiplying the cost/bag of soil by the number of bags needed. To determine the number of bags needed, first find the volume of the garden bed: $8\text{ ft} \times 6\text{ ft} \times 1.5\text{ ft} = 72$ cubic feet. Next, since each bag of sand contains 1.5 cubic feet of sand, the number of bags needed is $\frac{72\ cubic\ feet}{1.5\ cubic\ feet/bag} = 48$ bags. Finally, since the cost/bag is \$4.50, the cost for filling the sand box is \$4.50/bag × 48 bags = \$216.

Regents Practice Test #2

For questions 1–25, select the best answer from the answer choices.

1. In right triangle *ABC* below, what is the length of *AC*?

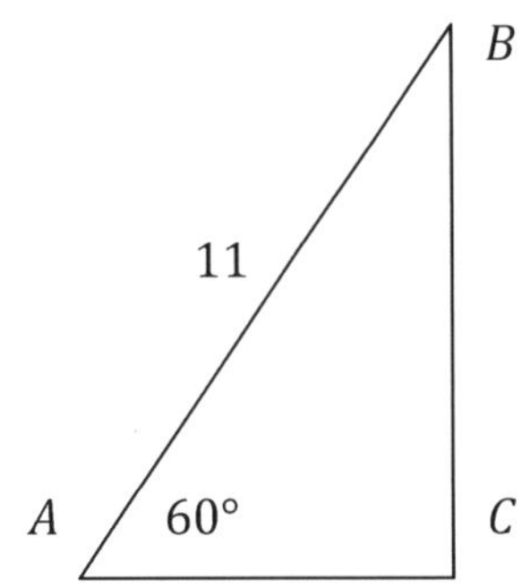

a. $\frac{11}{3}$
b. 5.5
c. $\frac{11\sqrt{3}}{2}$
d. $\frac{121\sqrt{3}}{8}$

2. In triangle *ABC* below, segment *CD* is a median. What is the length of *AB*?

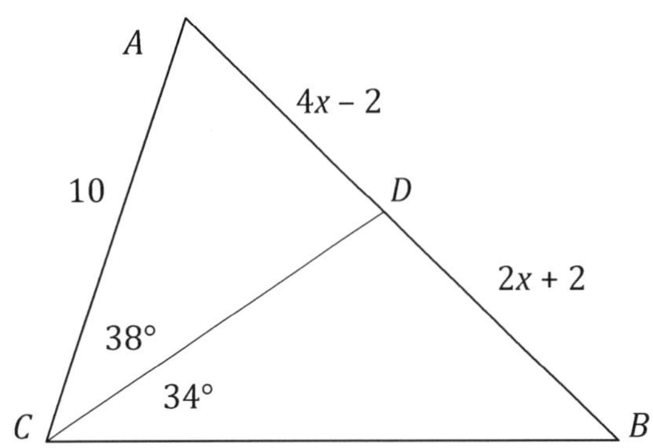

a. 2
b. 6
c. 12
d. 15

3. In the figure shown below, *JKLM* is a parallelogram. What is the measure of $\angle JKL$?

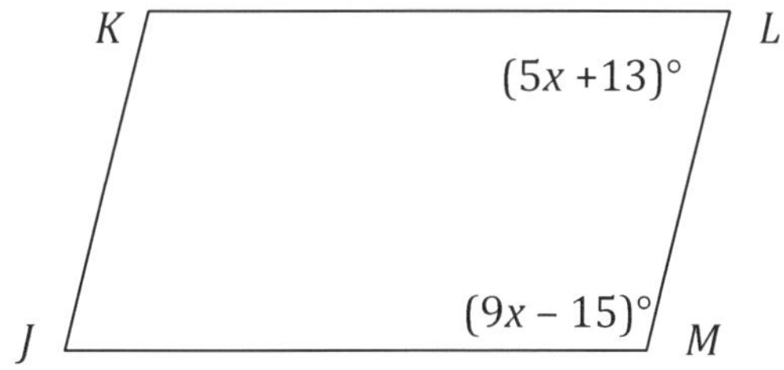

a. 13°
b. 44.1°
c. 78°
d. 102°

4. Segment *AB* goes through points *A* (1, –4) and *B* (–3, 2). Segment *CD* goes through points *C* (–3, –1) and *D* (6, 5). Segment *AB* is _______________ to Segment *CD*.

a. Parallel
b. Perpendicular
c. Tangent
d. Congruent

5. Given the line $y = -\frac{5}{2}x + 2$, find the equation of a line parallel to that line that passes through the point (2, 3).

a. $5x + 2y = 16$
b. $-2x + 5y = 11$
c. $-5x + 2y = -4$
d. $2x + 5y = 19$

6. In the figure below, lines *a* and *b* are parallel. Find the value of *x*.

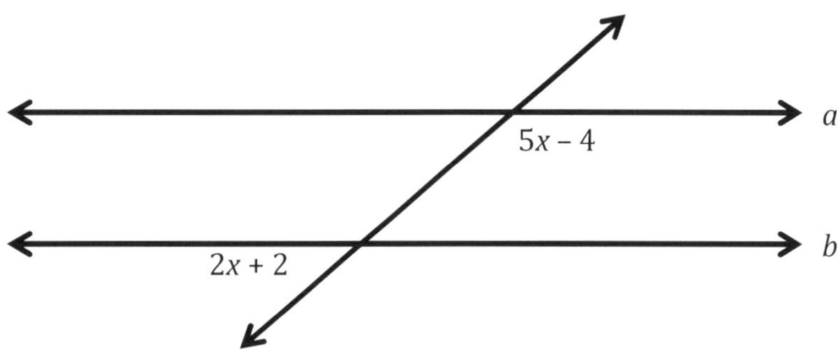

a. $x = 2$
b. $x = \frac{92}{7}$
c. $x = 26$
d. $x = 54$

7. In triangle ABC, shown below, point A is at (-2, 1), point B is at (6, 1), and point C is at (-2, -4). If the triangle is reflected across the x-axis, what are the new coordinates of point C?

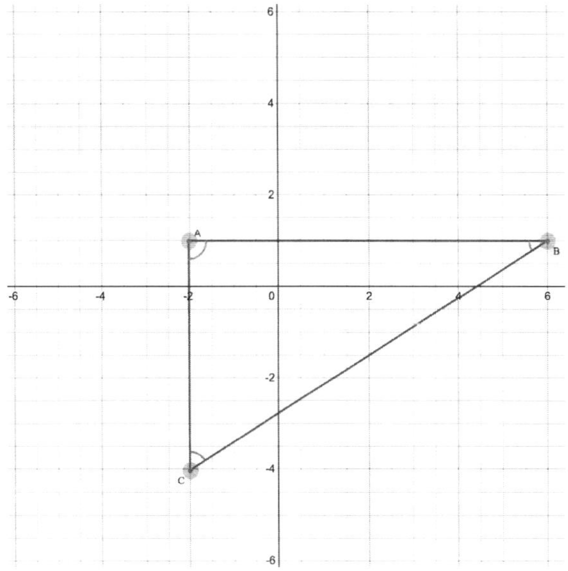

a. $(-2, 4)$
b. $(-2, -1)$
c. $(6, -1)$
d. $(2, -4)$

8. Which of the following sets of points creates a triangle that is congruent to the one from the previous problem?

a. $(-2, 0), (-10,0), (-2,6)$
b. $(-4, 0), (-4,8), (1,0)$
c. $(3, -1), (10, -1), (3,4)$
d. $(2, 2), (11,2), (2,8)$

9. In the figure below, line *l* is a transversal, intersecting parallel lines *A* and *B*. Complete line 6 in the proof that alternate exterior angles 1 and 8 are congruent.

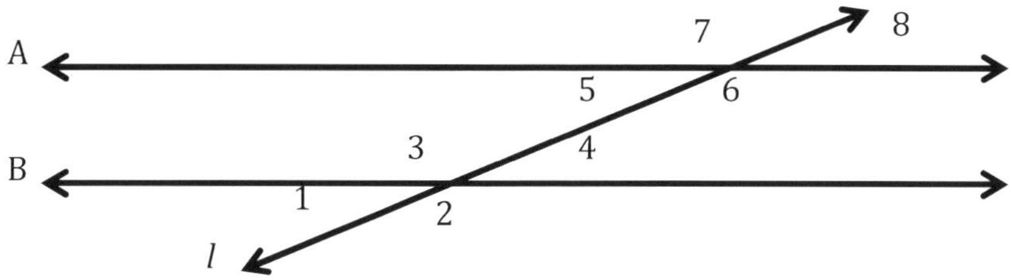

1.	Lines A and B are parallel	1.	Given
2.	Lines A and B cut by transversal l	2.	Given
3.	$\angle 1$ and $\angle 8$ are alternate exterior angles	3.	Definition of alternate exterior angles
4.	$\angle 1 \cong \angle 5, \angle 4 \cong \angle 8$	4.	Corresponding Angles Postulate
5.	$\angle 5 \cong \angle 8$	5.	Vertical Angles
6.	$\angle 1 \cong \angle 8$	6.	

a. Reflexive Property.
b. Symmetric Property.
c. Transitive Property.
d. CPCTC.

10. Rectangle *ABCD* is defined by the points *A* (–3, 0), *B* (–3, 10), *C* (2, 10), and *D* (2, 0). If it is dilated by a scale factor of $\frac{3}{5}$ to create its image *A′B′C′D′*, what is the length of *A′B′*?

a. 3
b. 6
c. 10
d. $\frac{50}{3}$

11. If the two right triangles below are similar, what is the hypotenuse of triangle *JKL*?

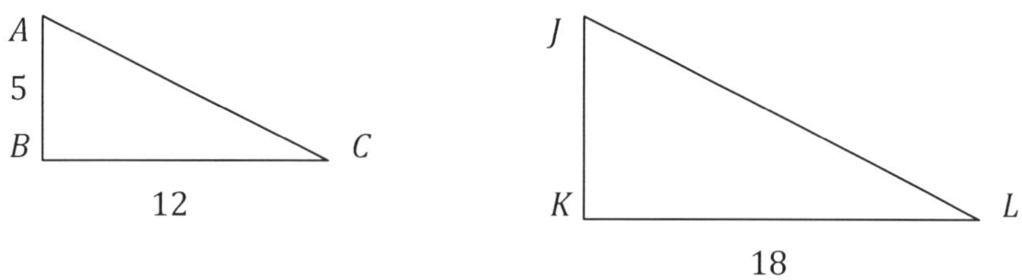

a. 7.5
b. 13
c. 19.5
d. 45

12. In ΔABC, if $\sin A = \cos 62°$, what is $\cos A$?

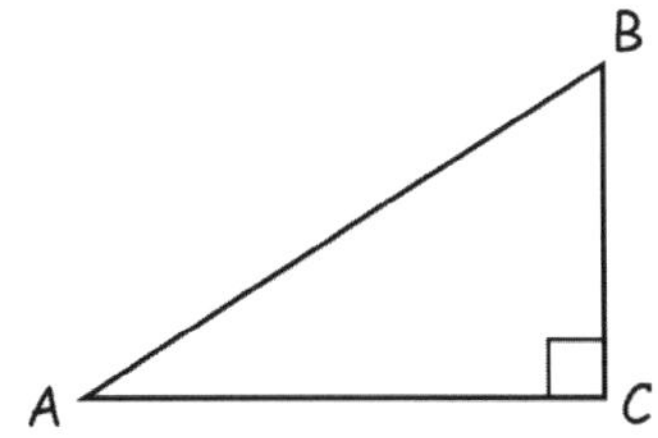

a. $\sin 28°$
b. $\sin 62°$
c. $\cos 62°$
d. $\sec 28°$

13. A jogging trail is in the shape of a right triangle. If it starts by going 600 m west, then goes 800 m north, then heads back to the start, what is the total distance of the trail?

a. 1,000 m
b. 1,400 m
c. 2,400 m
d. 240,000 m

14. Based on ΔPQR below, what is the value of x?

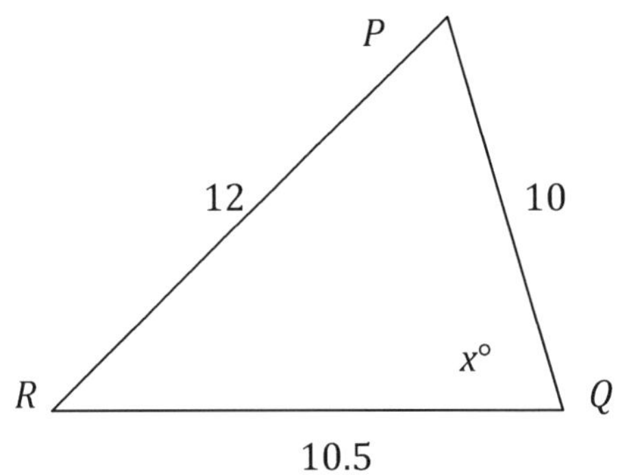

a. 71.6°
b. 67.3°
c. 56.1°
d. 52.3°

15. What is the length of the segment connecting the points (–8,2) and (4,–4)?

a. $6\sqrt{3}$
b. 12
c. $6\sqrt{5}$
d. 18

16. What are the coordinates of the midpoint of (-7, 3) and (2, -5)?

a. $(-5, -2)$
b. $\left(-\frac{5}{2}, 4\right)$
c. $\left(-\frac{5}{2}, -1\right)$
d. $\left(\frac{9}{2}, -1\right)$

17. A parallelogram is drawn on a coordinate plane. Its vertices are located at (-6, 2), (1, 2), (-2, -3), and (*x*, *y*). If (*x*, *y*) is located in Quadrant III, what are the coordinates of (*x*, *y*)?

a. (5, -3)
b. (-3, -3)
c. (-3, 7)
d. (-9, -3)

18. The vertices of an isosceles triangle are located at (-2, 6), (9, 1), and (-2, -4). What is the area of the triangle?

a. 110
b. 55
c. 34.17
d. 11

19. Circle A has an area of 144π cm². Circle B has an area of 225π cm². What is the ratio of the diameter of Circle A to the diameter of Circle B?

a. $\frac{4}{5}$
b. $\frac{16}{25}$
c. $\frac{5}{4}$
d. $\frac{25}{16}$

20. If a circle is inscribed in a square with sides of 16 cm, what is the area of the circle?

a. 16π cm²
b. $16\sqrt{2}\pi$ cm²
c. 64π cm²
d. 128π cm²

21. If Circle O below has a circumference of 18π in, what is the area of sector AOB?

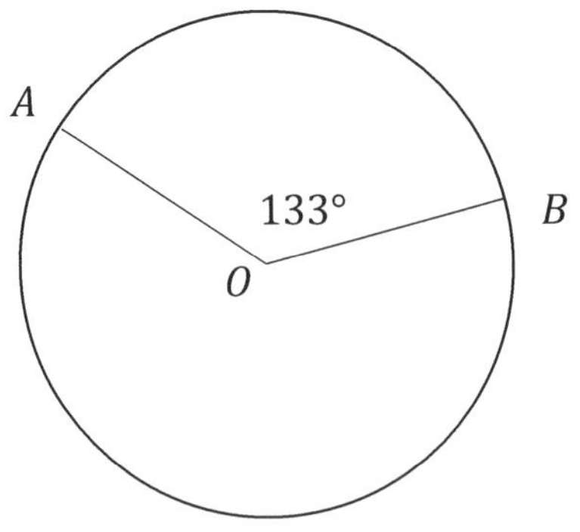

a. 20.88 in^2
b. 93.96 in^2
c. 254.34 in^2
d. 375.86 in^2

22. What is the center of the circle described by the equation $(x-7)^2+y^2-16=0$?

a. $(-7,-4)$
b. $(7,0)$
c. $(\frac{7}{2},4)$
d. $(-\frac{7}{2},0)$

23. What is the radius of the circle described by the equation $x^2+y^2-3x-8y=-12$?

a. $\frac{5}{2}$
b. 5
c. $\frac{25}{4}$
d. $2\sqrt{3}$

24. A water tower is in the shape of a cylinder with a diameter of 840 in and a height of 220 in. How much water can it hold when completely full?

a. $5.54x10^5$ in^3
b. $1.69x10^6$ in^3
c. $1.22x10^8$ in^3
d. $4.87x10^8$ in^3

25. The image below is the net of a cone. What is the cone's volume (figure not drawn to scale)?

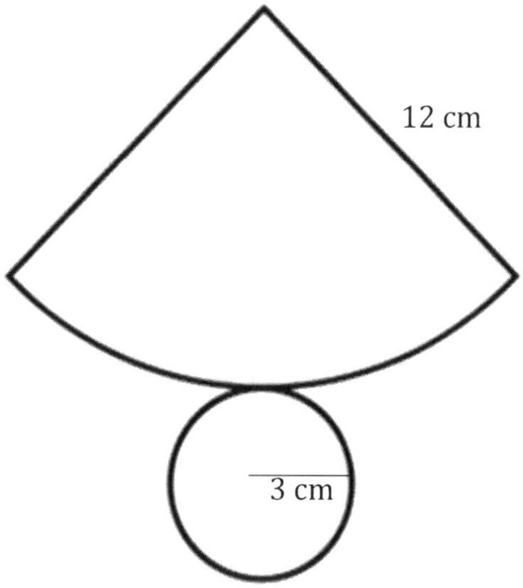

a. $9\sqrt{15}\pi\ \text{cm}^3$
b. $36\pi\ \text{cm}^3$
c. $27\sqrt{15}\pi\ \text{cm}^3$
d. $45\pi\ \text{cm}^3$

For questions 26–35, select one or more answers from the answer choices.

26. Which of the following pairs of triangles can be proved to be congruent by ASA?

a.
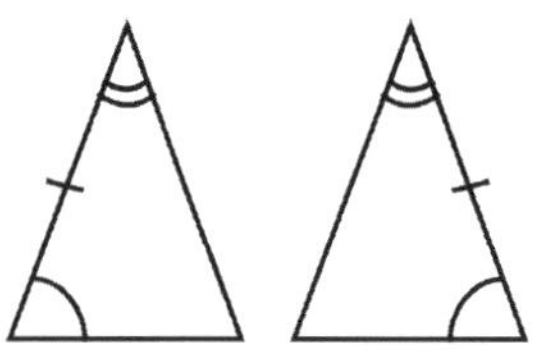

b.
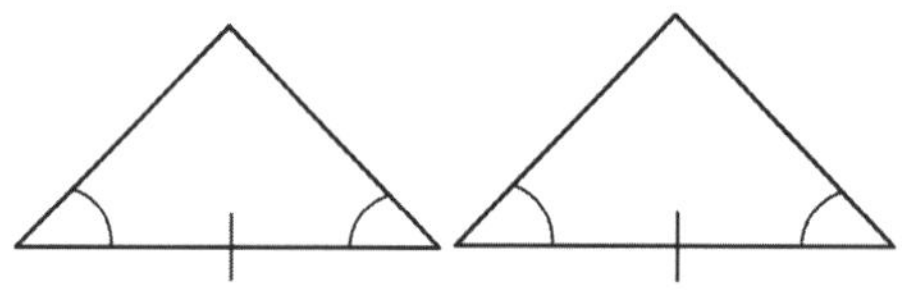

c.
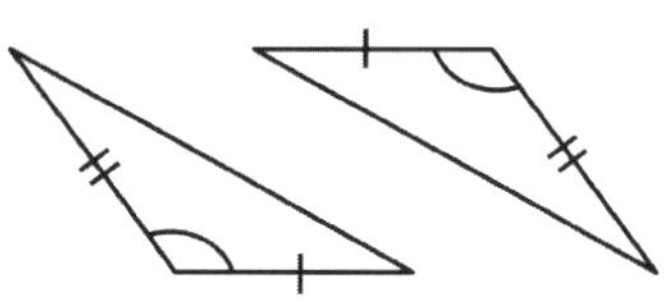

d.
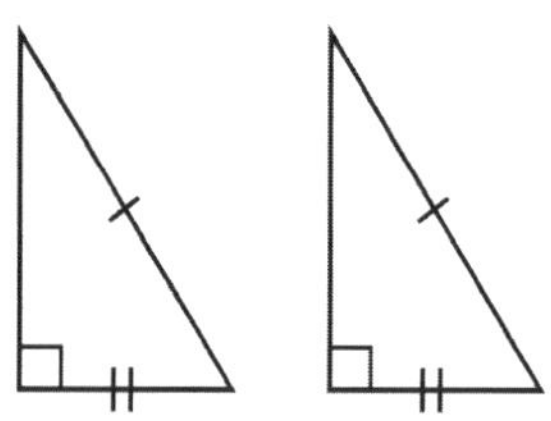

27. The following steps describe the construction of a polygon. Which shape(s) are possible?

Step 1 – Draw a line segment with a straightedge.
Step 2 – Place a compass point on one end of the line segment and measure the distance to the other end. With the compass fixed, draw an arc from the endpoint, curving above the segment.
Step 3 – Keeping the compass fixed, draw an arc from the other endpoint, also curving above the segment.
Step 4 – From the point of intersection of the two arcs, draw a line segment to each of the endpoints of the original segment.

a. Equilateral Triangle
b. Right Triangle
c. Isosceles Triangle
d. Square

28. Two square pyramids are similar. If Pyramid A has a base length of 8 cm and a height between 10 and 12 cm, and Pyramid B has a base length of 6 cm, which of the following choices could be possible volume(s) of Pyramid B?

a. 84
b. 92
c. 97.73
d. 107.5

29. Sin 137° is equivalent to which of the following values?

a. sin 43°
b. cos 43°
c. sin 223°
d. cos 313°

30. Quadrilateral *ABCD* has vertices at (−1,3), (2,5), (4,2), and (1,0). What shape is it?

a. Square
b. Rectangle
c. Parallelogram
d. Rhombus

31. A circle has a diameter of 16*c* inches. What is the area?

a. $16\pi c$ in
b. $64\pi c^2$ in^2
c. $\frac{4\pi c^2}{9}$ ft^2
d. $\frac{16\pi c^2}{3}$ ft^2

32. A circle has a center at (0, 0) and passes through the point $(2\sqrt{3}, 2)$. Which of the following points also lie(s) on the circle?

a. $(0, -3.5)$
b. $(-4, 0)$
c. $(-\sqrt{3}, -3)$
d. $(-2\sqrt{2}, 2\sqrt{2})$

33. A circle has a diameter of 8 and a center at $(3, -4)$. Which of the following equations describe(s) that circle?

a. $(x-3)^2 + (y+4)^2 = 64$
b. $x^2 - 6x + y^2 + 8y + 9 = 0$
c. $x^2 + y^2 - 6x + 8y - 8 = -17$
d. $(x+3)^2 + 9 + (y-4)^2 - 2 = 34$

34. A cylinder has a diameter of 12 m and a height of 9 m. What is the cylinder's surface area?

a. $5.65x10^7$ cm²
b. $1.58x10^9$ mm²
c. $1.58x10^{-3}$ km²
d. $5.65x10^2$ m²

35. Which of the following are possible two-dimensional shapes that can be formed from the various cross-sections of a square pyramid?

a. Triangle
b. Square
c. Trapezoid
d. Pentagon

For questions 36–50, enter a numerical answer.

36. In triangle *ABC* below, side *AB* = 4*x* and side *BC* = 6*x* – $2\sqrt{2}$. What is the length of *AC*?

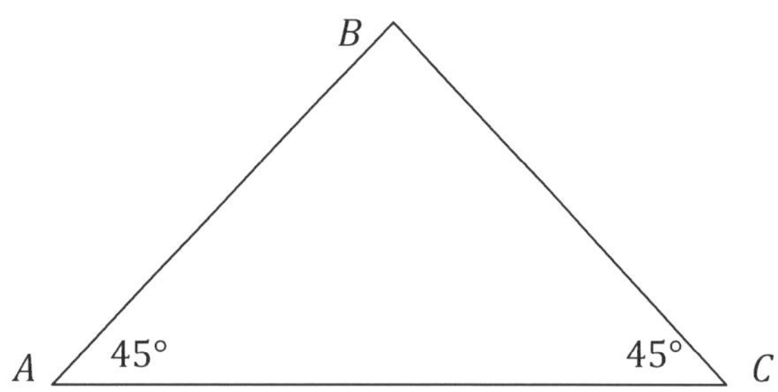

37. A building's layout is shaped like a trapezoid as seen below. What is the total perimeter of the building in feet? All angles that appear to be right are right.

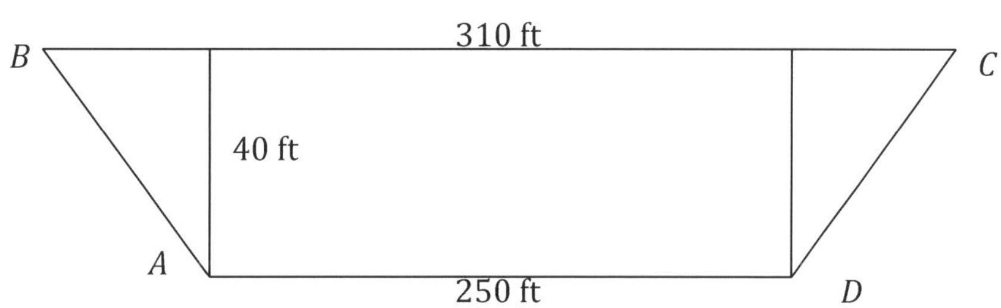

38. Right triangles *ABC* and *DEF* below are congruent. If *AB* is 15, *AC* is $3x+3$ and *DF* is $5x-1$, what is the area of triangle *DEF*?

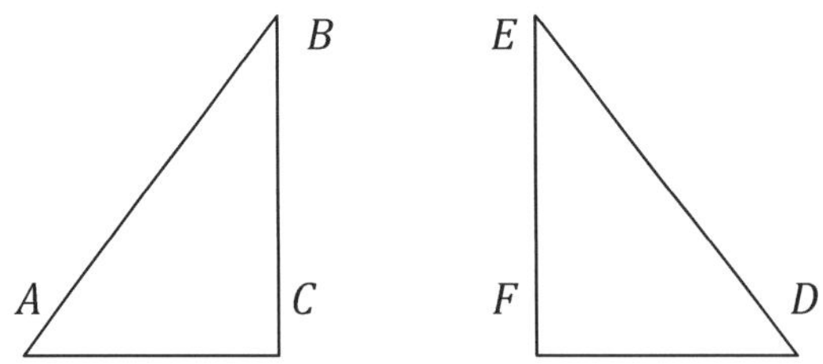

39. If triangle *MNP* below is dilated by a factor of $\frac{5}{3}$ to become triangle *QRS*, what is the measure of angle *Q*?

40. A child lies on the ground 50 feet from the base of a tree. If the child looks up at an angle of elevation of 38° to see a bird in the tree, how high up is the bird? Round answer to the nearest foot.

41. In Triangle JKL below, what is the length of JK? Round to the nearest whole unit.

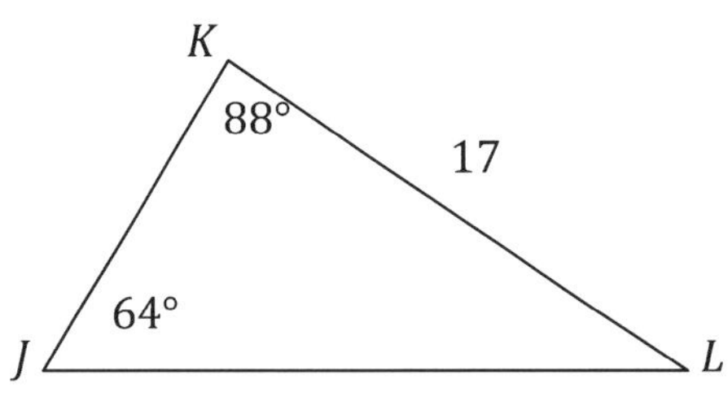

42. **If triangle *ABC* is defined by the points *A* (0, 4), *B* (−2, 7), and *C* (6, −8), what is the length of *BC*?**

43. **Find the perimeter of the trapezoid defined by the points (0, 2), (3, 2), (7, −1), and (−4, −1).**

44. **Find the central angle of a circle if the arc length is 12 inches and the area is 81π square inches (round to the nearest whole degree).**

45. **Quadrilateral *ABCD* is inscribed in a circle as seen below. Arc *ABC* is $10x - 2$. Angle *D* is $4x + 15$. What is the measure of $\angle D$?**

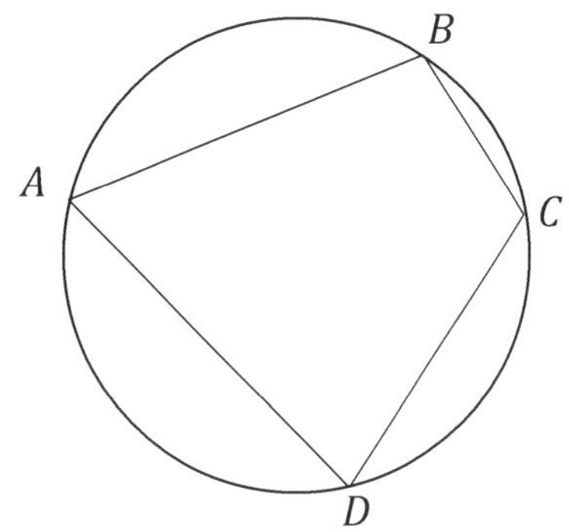

46. **On Circle *O* below, segment *PQ* is tangent to the circle at point *L*. If the diameter of the circle is 30 and *OP* is 25, what is the length of *PQ*?**

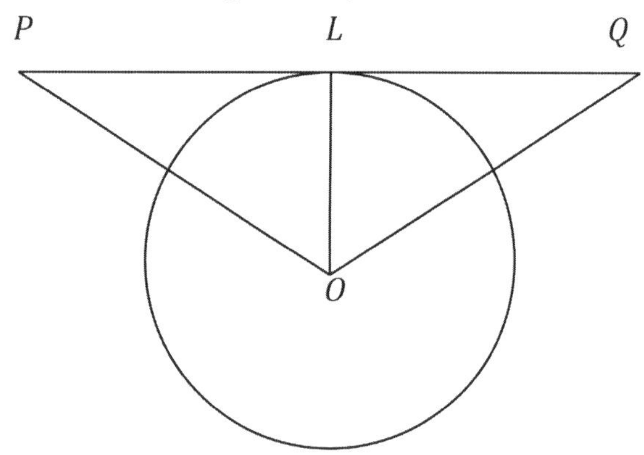

47. The sides of quadrilateral *JKLM* are tangent to the circle. What is the length of *KL*?

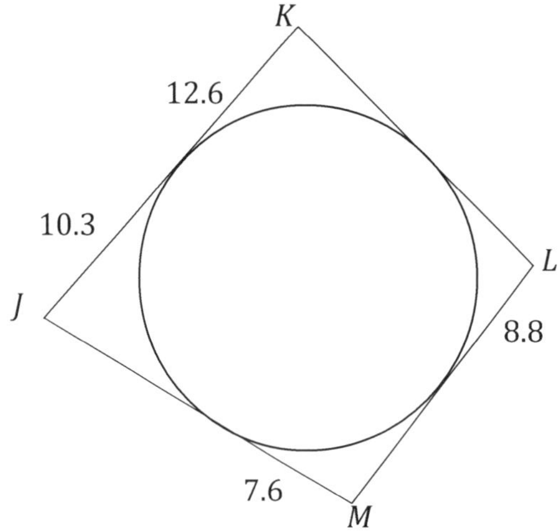

48. What is the area of the darker shaded sector in the circle below, rounded to the nearest square inch?

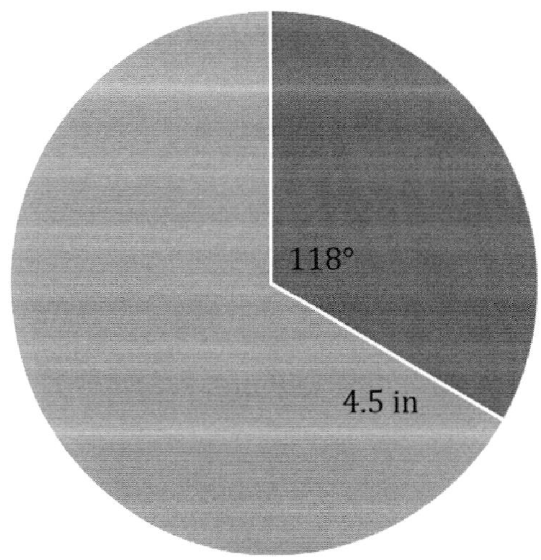

49. The surface area of a rectangular prism is 576 cubic centimeters. If a similar prism is created but each side is $\frac{1}{2}$ the length of the corresponding side in the first prism, what is the surface area of the new prism?

50. Jordan is building a cylindrical tank to hold water. He wants it to hold 150 gallons. If the radius of the tank is 18 inches, how high does it need to be, rounded to the nearest inch (1 gallon = 231 cubic inches)?

Answer Key and Explanations for Test #2

1. B: Since we are told that this is a right triangle, we know that angle C is 90°. Thus, angle B must be 30°, so this is a 30-60-90 triangle. This is a special triangle: the ratio of the shortest leg to the hypotenuse is always $\frac{1}{2}$. So, AC is half of AB: $\frac{11}{2} = 5.5$. Choice A divides the hypotenuse by 3 instead of 2. Choice C gives side BC. Choice D gives the area of the triangle.

2. C: In a triangle, a median bisects a side of the triangle, even though it may not be an angle bisector. So, we know that AD and BD are the same length and can set them equal to each other: $4x - 2 = 2x + 2$. We subtract $2x$ from each side and add 2 to each side: $2x = 4$. Dividing each side by 2 yields $x = 2$. Then we can solve for either segment: $AD = 4(2) - 2 = 6$. Since BD is also 6, AB is $6 + 6 = 12$. Answer A is the value of x. Answer B is the value of AD or BD.

3. D: One of the theorems about parallelograms states that the adjacent angles in a parallelogram are supplementary. Therefore, according to the figure, $\angle KLM + \angle LMJ = 180$, so $5x + 13 + 9x - 15 = 180$. We combine like terms to find that $14x = 182$. Dividing both sides by 14 yields $x = 13$. Another theorem about parallelograms states that the opposite angles in a parallelogram are equal. Thus, $\angle JKL = \angle LMJ$. To find the measure of $\angle LMJ$, we first substitute the value for x into the expression for $\angle LMJ$: $9(13) - 15 = 117 - 15 = 102°$. Answer A is the value of x. Answer B is the measure of $\angle JKL$ if the angles were incorrectly thought to be complementary instead of supplementary. Answer C is the value of $\angle KLM$.

4. B: We check the slopes and the lengths of the segments to see how they compare. We find the slope of Segment AB by dividing the difference in y-values by the difference in x-values: $m = \frac{2-(-4)}{-3(-1)} = \frac{6}{-4} = -\frac{3}{2}$. We then find the slope of Segment CD: $m = \frac{5-(-1)}{6-(-3)} = \frac{6}{9} = \frac{2}{3}$. Next we find the length of each by using the distance formula from one point to another: $AB = \sqrt{(1-(-3))^2 + (-4-2)^2} = \sqrt{4^2 + (-6)^2} = \sqrt{16+36} = \sqrt{52}$, and $CD = \sqrt{(-3-6)^2 + (-1-5)^2} = \sqrt{(-9)^2 + (-6)^2} = \sqrt{81+36} = \sqrt{117}$. We can see from the slopes that they are opposite reciprocals, so the segments are perpendicular. Parallel segments (Answer A) would have had identical slopes. Congruent segments (Answer D) would have been the same length. A tangent segment or line (Answer C) is one that just touches a curve without passing through it.

5. A: The slope of the original line is $m = -\frac{5}{2}$. Since the new line needs to be parallel, the new slope needs to be the same as the original slope. The given point is (2, 3), which is equivalent to (x_1, y_1) in the point-slope equation of $y - y_1 = m(x - x_1)$. Substituting in the new slope and given point, the point-slope equation becomes $y - 3 = -\frac{5}{2}(x - 2)$. Distributing on the right side of the equation results in $y - 3 = -\frac{5}{2}x + 5$. Add 3 to both sides of the equation to get the parallel line of $y = -\frac{5}{2}x + 8$. Multiplying through by 2 and moving the x-value to the left yields: $5x + 2y = 16$. Answer B found the perpendicular line. Answer C used the opposite slope. Answer D took the reciprocal slope.

6. C: The listed angles are supplementary angles. When a transversal cuts across parallel lines, the alternate interior angles are congruent, but an interior angle and its alternate exterior angle are supplementary. Since lines a and b are parallel, it means that $5x - 4 + 2x + 2 = 180$. Combining like terms and moving constants to the right yields $7x = 182$, or $x = 26$. In Answer A, the angles were incorrectly treated as equal. In Answer B, the angles were incorrectly treated as complementary. Answer D is the measure of the lower left angle rather than the value of x.

7. A: Reflecting a point across the x-axis involves leaving the x-coordinate as it is and switching the sign of the y-coordinate. Answer B is the reflection of point A. Answer C is the reflection of point B. Answer D is the reflection of point C across the y-axis.

8. B: In order for two figures to be congruent, they must have the same size and shape. The triangle from the previous problem is a right triangle with legs of 8 and 5, so we test the points in the answer choices to see which one matches by finding the difference in x- and y-values in the coordinates. Answer A has legs of 8 and 6. Answer C has legs of 7 and 5. Answer D has legs of 9 and 6. Only Answer B has a triangle with legs of 8 and 5, congruent to the one from the previous problem.

9. C: The property that a value can be substituted for another value that has already been determined to be congruent is termed the transitive property. The reflexive property (Answer A) states that a segment or angle is congruent to itself. The symmetric property (Answer B) states that if $a = b$, then $b = a$. CPCTC (Answer D) stands for "Corresponding Parts of Congruent Triangles are Congruent," which does not apply to this proof since it does not involve triangles.

10. B: We first find the length of side AB in the original rectangle. From point (–3, 0) to (–3, 10) is a distance of 10. So, the dilated length can be found by multiplying the scale factor: $10 \cdot \frac{3}{5} = 6$. Answer A is the length of $B'C'$ or $D'A'$. Answer C is the length of AB without dilation. Answer D divided by $\frac{3}{5}$ instead of multiplying.

11. C: Since we know that the two triangles are similar, we know that the ratio of each side to its corresponding side in the other triangle is the same. So, we can solve for side JK by setting up a ratio: $\frac{12}{18} = \frac{5}{JK}$. Then we cross-multiply: $12JK = 5(18)$, or $JK = \frac{5(18)}{12} = 7.5$. Then we can solve for the hypotenuse, JL, by using the **Pythagorean theorem**: $7.5^2 + 18^2 = JL^2$, or $380.25 = JL^2$. We take the square root of each side to find that JL is 19.5. Answer A is the length of side JK. Answer B is the length of side AC. Answer D is the perimeter of triangle JKL.

12. B: The sine function is represented by the ratio $\frac{opposite\ leg}{hypotenuse}$. So, the sine of angle A can be written as $\frac{BC}{AB}$. The cosine function is represented by the ratio $\frac{adjacent\ leg}{hypotenuse}$. In ΔABC, cos B can also be written as $\frac{BC}{AB}$. We can also determine that angle B is 62°. Since the two acute angles of a right triangle are complementary, we can find that angle A is $90 - 62 = 28°$. Since we can see that the sine of angle A is equal to the cosine of angle B, we know that the cosine of angle A will also be equal to the sine of angle B. So $\cos A = \sin B = \sin 62°$. Answer A incorrectly set $\cos A = \sin A$. Answer C incorrectly set $\cos A = \cos B$. Answer D set $\cos A = \sec A$, which is incorrect because secant is the reciprocal of cosine.

13. C: We are given two legs of a right triangle and need to find the hypotenuse so that we can then find the perimeter (total distance of the trail). We use the **Pythagorean theorem** to find the hypotenuse: $600^2 + 800^2 = h^2$, or $h = \sqrt{600^2 + 800^2} = \sqrt{360{,}000 + 640{,}000} = \sqrt{1{,}000{,}000} = 1000$. So, we can find the total distance, or perimeter, by adding the three sides of the triangle: $600 + 800 + 1000 = 2400$. Thus, the trail is 2,400 m long. Answer A is the length of the hypotenuse. Answer B is the length of the two legs together. Answer D is the area of the triangle rather than the perimeter.

14. A: In the figure, since we have all three sides but no angles, we need to use the Law of Cosines to solve for x. The Law of Cosines is $c^2 = a^2 + b^2 - 2ab\cos(C)$. If we let $a = 10$, $b = 10.5$ and $c = 12$, then the Law of Cosines becomes $12^2 = 10^2 + 10.5^2 - 2(10)(10.5)\cos x$. We isolate x by first moving the constants to the left: $12^2 - 10^2 - 10.5^2 = -2(10)(10.5)\cos x$. We then simply the left side: $144 - 100 - 110.25 = -2(10)(10.5)\ \cos x$, or $-66.25 = -2(10)(10.5)\cos x$. Finally, we divide by $-2(10)(10.5)$: $\frac{-66.25}{-2(10)(10.5)} = \cos x$, or $\cos x = 0.31548$. We then take the arccosine of each side to solve for x: $\arccos(\cos x) = \arccos 0.31548$, or $x = 71.6°$. Answer C is the measure of $\angle RPQ$. Answer D is the measure of $\angle QRP$.

15. C: To calculate distance between points, the distance formula can be used: $d = \sqrt{(x_1 - x_2)^2 + (y_1 - y_2)^2}$. We can use the points $(-8, 2)$ and $(4, -4)$ for the x- and y-values: $\sqrt{(-8-4)^2 + (2 - -4)^2} = \sqrt{(-12)^2 + 6^2} = \sqrt{144 + 36} = \sqrt{180} = 6\sqrt{5}$. Answer A uses the **Pythagorean theorem** (which is what the distance formula actually is, finding the difference in x- and y-values and using those as the legs of a right triangle) but uses the x-values as the hypotenuse instead of a leg. Answer B is the difference in the x-values. Answer D is the difference in the x-values plus the difference in the y-values.

16. C: The midpoint between two points is simply the average of the x-values and the y-values. So, we can calculate the midpoint of (-7, 3) and (2, -5): $\left(\frac{-7+2}{2}, \frac{3-5}{2}\right) = (-\frac{5}{2}, -1)$. Answer A added the points but did not divide by 2. Answer B treated all of the y-coordinates as positive. Answer D treated all of the x-coordinates as positive.

17. D: We can plot the three points on a coordinate plane and call point (-6, 2) A, point (1, 2) B, point (-2, -3) C, and point (x, y) D, which is in Quadrant III. Because it is a parallelogram, opposite sides must be parallel, so we can say that side BC is parallel to side DA. Thus, these two segments will have the same slope. The slope of segment BC can be found from the points: $\frac{2-(-3)}{1-(-2)} = \frac{5}{3}$, as moving from point C to point B requires moving up 5 and over 3. So, the slope of line DA will also be $\frac{5}{3}$, and moving from point D to point A can also be described as moving up 5 and over 3. As point A is (-6, 2), we subtract 3 from the x-coordinate and 5 from the y-coordinate to find that point D is (-9, -3). Answer A would be the fourth point if it were located in Quadrant IV instead of Quadrant III. Answer B adds 3 to the x-coordinate instead of subtracting, creating a trapezoid. Answer C adds 3 to the x-coordinate and 5 to the y-coordinate instead of subtracting both.

18. B: We can plot the three points on the coordinate plane and find the height and base to determine the area. From point (-2, 6) to point (-2, -4) there is a vertical distance of 10. This is the base of the triangle. From the midpoint of this segment, (-2, 1), to point (9, 1) there is a horizontal distance of 11. So, the triangle has a base of 10 and a height of 11. The area of a triangle can be found by the formula $A = \frac{1}{2}bh$, or $\frac{1}{2}(10)(11) = \frac{110}{2} = 55$. Answer A is the area without dividing by 2. Answer C is the perimeter of the triangle. Answer D is the height of the triangle.

19. A: The area of each circle can be found by the formula $A = \pi r^2$. So, we can find the radius of Circle A by dividing the area by π and then taking the square root: $r = \sqrt{\frac{144\pi}{\pi}} = \sqrt{144} = 12$. The diameter is twice the radius, or 24. We do the same for Circle B to find a radius of 15 and diameter of 30. To find the ratio, we divide Circle A's diameter by Circle B's diameter: $\frac{24}{30} = \frac{4}{5}$. Answer B is the ratio of the area of Circle A to Circle B. Answer C is the ratio of the diameter of Circle B to Circle A. Answer D is the ratio of the area of Circle B to Circle A.

20. C: If a circle is inscribed in a square, the length of the side of the square is the length of the diameter. So, the radius of the circle is 8 cm. We can then calculate the area as $A = \pi r^2 = \pi(8)^2 = 64\pi$. Answer A is the circumference of the circle. Answer B is the circumference if the square is inscribed in the circle. Answer D is the area if the square is inscribed in the circle.

21. B: The area of the sector of a circle is calculated using the equation: $\frac{Central\ Angle\ Measure}{360°} \times \pi r^2$, where r is the radius of the circle. If the circumference of the circle is 18 π in, we can find the radius: $C = 2\pi r$, so $r = \frac{C}{2\pi} = \frac{18\pi}{2\pi} = 9$ in. Since the central angle measure is 133°, the equation becomes: $\frac{133°}{360°} \times \pi(9\ in)^2 = 93.96\ in^2$. Answer A found the length of arc AB. Answer C is the area of the circle. Answer D used the diameter length instead of the radius in the calculation.

22. B: We adjust this equation to standard form: $(x - 7)^2 + (y - 0)^2 = 4^2$. The center can be found by setting each parenthetical term equal to zero: $x - 7 = 0 \Rightarrow x = 7$, so the x-coordinate of the center is 7. The y-coordinate is: $y - 0 = 0 \Rightarrow y = 0$. So, the center is at $(7, 0)$. Answer A reverses the sign of the x-value and takes the root of the constant next to the y-value. Answer C halves the x-value and takes the root of the constant next to the y-value. Answer D halves the x-value and changes the sign, but uses the correct y-value.

23. A: We begin by isolating x- and y-terms and completing the square: $x^2 - 3x + \frac{9}{4} + y^2 - 8y + 16 = -12 + \frac{9}{4} + 16$. This simplifies to: $\left(x - \frac{3}{2}\right)^2 + (y - 4)^2 = \frac{25}{4}$. The radius is the root of the variable on the right side of the equal sign when the equation is in this format, so $r = \sqrt{\frac{25}{4}} = \frac{5}{2}$. Answer B is the diameter. Answer C is the radius squared. Answer D takes the value to the right of the equal sign in the original equation as the radius squared (ignoring the sign).

24. C: We calculate volume of a cylinder with the following formula: $V = \pi r^2 h$, where r is the radius and h is the height. The radius is half of the given diameter, or 420 in, so $V = \pi(420)^2(220) = 121{,}857{,}120$. We can write this in scientific notation by moving the decimal to the left 8 places: $1.22x10^8$ in^3. Answer A is the area of the base of the water tower. Answer B is the surface area of the water tower. Answer D is the volume using the value of the diameter as the radius.

25. A: We can calculate the volume of a cone as follows: $V = \frac{1}{3}\pi r^2 h$. We know that the radius is 3 cm, but we need to find the height. We can use the radius and the slant height to create a right triangle as pictured below:

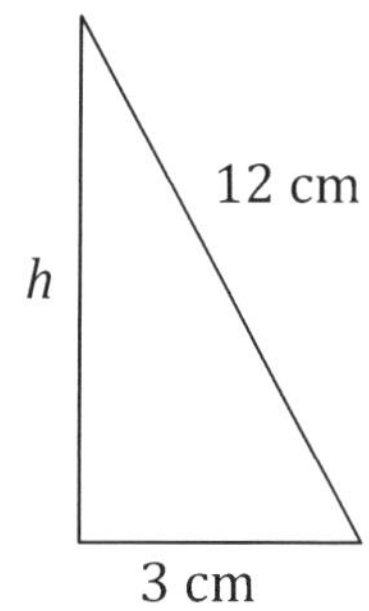

We then use the Pythagorean theorem to calculate the height: $h^2 + 3^2 = 12^2$, or $h = \sqrt{12^2 - 3^2} = \sqrt{144 - 9} = \sqrt{135} = 3\sqrt{15}$. Now we can calculate the volume: $V = \frac{1}{3}\pi(3)^2(3\sqrt{15}) = \frac{27\sqrt{15}\pi}{3} = 9\sqrt{15}\pi$. Answer B is the volume when using the slant height instead of the real height. Answer C is the volume without dividing by 3. Answer D is the surface area of the cone.

26. A, B: ASA stands for "Angle Side Angle," and can be used to prove that two triangles are similar when two sides, along with the angle between the two sides, are similar in both triangles. Answers A and B each have two pairs of congruent angles, along with the side between these two angles, so they can be proven to be congruent by ASA. Answer C has two triangles that are congruent by SAS (Side Angle Side). Answer D has two right triangles that are congruent by HL (Hypotenuse Leg).

27. A, C: The listed steps describe the construction of an equilateral triangle, drawing one side and then constructing two other sides of equal length. An equilateral triangle cannot be a right triangle (Answer B) since all three angles must be 60°, but it can be an isosceles triangle, since isosceles means two equal sides and any two sides of an equilateral triangle are equal. It is not a four-sided square (Answer D).

28. B, C, D: If Pyramid A has a square base with sides of 8 cm and Pyramid B has a square base with sides of 6 cm, we can find the ratio between the two triangles: $\frac{A}{B} = \frac{8}{6} = \frac{4}{3}$. So we can plug in the low and high potential heights of Pyramid A to find the height range for Pyramid B: $\frac{A}{B} = \frac{4}{3} = \frac{10}{h_1} \Rightarrow 4h_1 = 3(10) \Rightarrow h_1 = 7.5$, and $\frac{A}{B} = \frac{4}{3} = \frac{12}{h_2} \Rightarrow 4h_2 = 3(12) \Rightarrow h_2 = 9$. So, Pyramid B has a height between 7.5 and 9. Thus we can find the smallest possible volume of Pyramid B: $V = \frac{1}{3}bh = \frac{1}{3}(6)^2(7.5) = 90$. The largest possible volume of Pyramid B is: $V = \frac{1}{3}bh = \frac{1}{3}(6)^2(9) = 108$. So, any value between 90 and 108 is a possible volume of Pyramid B.

29. A, D: The sine of one angle is equivalent to the cosine of the complementary angle. Since 137° is 43° above the y-axis (180 - 137 = 43), then this is the equivalent of sin 43° or cos 47° (90 - 43 = 47). Cos 313° is the equivalent of cos 47° because 313° is 47° below the y-axis and cosine is positive in Quadrant IV. Answer B is incorrect because it did not take the complementary angle. Answer C is incorrect because sine is negative in Quadrant III.

30. A, B, C, D: We can plot the four points and draw the quadrilateral, then find the length and slope of each side to see what kind it is. Let point A be (-1,3), point B be (2,5), point C be (4,2) and point D be (1,0). We find the length of each side by using the distance formula. Side AB has a length of $\sqrt{(-1-2)^2 + (3-5)^2} = \sqrt{13}$ and a slope of $\frac{5-3}{2--1} = \frac{2}{3}$. Side BC has a length of $\sqrt{(2-4)^2 + (5-2)^2} = \sqrt{13}$ and a slope of $\frac{2-5}{4-2} = -\frac{3}{2}$. Side CD has a length of

$\sqrt{(4-1)^2+(2-0)^2}=\sqrt{13}$ and a slope of $\frac{0-2}{1-4}=\frac{2}{3}$. Side DA has a length of $\sqrt{(1--1)^2+(0-3)^2}=\sqrt{13}$ and a slope of $\frac{3-0}{-1-1}=-\frac{3}{2}$. Since AB and CD have the same length and slope, and BC and DA also have the same length and slope, we have two pairs of parallel sides, meaning it is a parallelogram (C). The sides are all the same length, so it is a rhombus (D). To determine if it is a square (A) or rectangle (B), we need to know if the angles are right angles. If they are, the slopes of adjacent sides will be perpendicular. In other words, the slopes will be opposite reciprocals of each other. The two slopes are $-\frac{3}{2}$ and $\frac{2}{3}$, which are opposite reciprocals, so the shape is both a rectangle (two pairs of parallel sides with 90° angles) and a square (two pairs of parallel sides of equal length with 90° angles).

31. B, C: The formula for the area of a circle is $A=\pi r^2$. If the diameter is $16c$, then the radius is $8c$, so we can calculate area: $A=\pi(8c)^2=64\pi c^2\text{ in}^2$. This can be converted to feet by dividing the radius by 12: $A=\pi\left(\frac{2}{3}c\right)^2=\frac{4\pi c^2}{9}\text{ ft}^2$. Answer A is the circumference of the circle. Answer D divides the area in inches by 12 rather than dividing the radius by 12 before squaring.

32. B, D: A circle centered at (0, 0) that passes through the point $(2\sqrt{3},2)$ has a radius, r, of 4 units, since $r=\sqrt{\left(0-2\sqrt{3}\right)^2+(0-2)^2}=\sqrt{\left(2\sqrt{3}\right)^2+(2)^2}=\sqrt{12+4}=\sqrt{16}=4$. The equation for a circle with a center of (0, 0) and $r=4$ is $(x-0)^2+(y-0)^2=4^2$, which simplifies as $x^2+y^2=16$. We try out the answer choices one by one to see if they work, substituting the points from the answer choices into the circle equation:

Answer A: $0^2+(-3.5)^2=12.25$.

Answer B: $(-4)^2+(0)^2=16$.

Answer C: $(-\sqrt{3})^2+(-3)^2=3+9=12$.

Answer D: $\left(-2\sqrt{2}\right)^2+\left(2\sqrt{2}\right)^2=8+8=16$.

Answers B and D fit the equation, so these are points on the circle.

33. B, C: The equation for a circle is $(x-h)^2+(y-k)^2=r^2$, where (h,k) is the center of the circle and r is the radius. Since the center of the circle is $(3,-4)$ and the radius is half of the diameter $(8\div 2=4)$, those values can be substituted into the equation as $(x-3)^2+(y-(-4))^2=4^2$ which is equal to $(x-3)^2+(y+4)^2=16$. We can expand it to $x^2-6x+9+y^2+8y+16=16$, or $x^2-6x+y^2+8y=-9$. We then check the answers to any that are equivalent to this:

Answer A squares the diameter instead of the radius, so it is not a match.

Answer B matches the expanded form above.

Answer C has a constant on the left side of the equation, –8. When this is subtracted from the –17 on the right $(-17-(-8)=-9)$, it matches the expanded form above.

Answer D switches the signs of the constants inside the parentheses and the constants outside the parentheses do not add to 16 when moved to the right, so it is not a match.

34. D: The formula for the surface area of a cylinder is $SA=2\pi r^2+2\pi rh$, where r is the radius and h is the height. Since the cylinder has a diameter of 12 m, the radius is half of the diameter, or 6 m.

The height is 9 m. Therefore, $SA = 2\pi(6\ m)^2 + 2\pi(6m)(9\ m)$= 565.2 m² or $5.65x10^2$ m^2. This can be converted to other units. To convert to centimeters (Answer A), multiply by 100^2 to obtain $5.65x10^6$ cm³. To convert to millimeters (Answer B), multiply by $1{,}000^2$ to obtain $5.65x10^8$ mm^3. To convert to kilometers, divide by $1{,}000^2$ to obtain $5.65x10^{-4}$ km^3. Answer A does not have the correct number of decimal places. Answers B and C used the diameter in place of the radius.

35. A, B, C: When a cross-section is taken of a square pyramid, it can form a triangle if taken through the vertex at the top, perpendicular to the base. If taken parallel to the base, it forms a square. If taken at an angle through the sides, it can be a trapezoid. A four-sided pentagon is impossible.

36. The correct answer is 8: Since angles *A* and *C* are each 45°, we know that angle *B* must be 90° (180 – 45 – 45 = 90). So, this is a 45-45-90 special triangle. The short legs are equal to each other and the length of the hypotenuse is the length of a short leg times $\sqrt{2}$. To find the short legs, we set *AB* and *BC* equal to each other: $4x = 6x - 2\sqrt{2}$. We subtract 6*x* from both sides: $-2x = -2\sqrt{2}$. Finally, we divide each side by –2 to yield: $x = \sqrt{2}$. We can plug this value into the equation for either leg to find that $AB = BC = 4\sqrt{2}$. To find *AC*, we multiply this by $\sqrt{2}$: $4\sqrt{2} \cdot \sqrt{2} = 4(2) = 8$.

37. The correct answer is 660: To find the perimeter of the figure, we need to find the length of the unknown sides. Figure *ABCD* is a trapezoid, or a rectangle with two right triangles attached. We can subtract the length of *AD* from *BC* and divide by 2 to find the length of each short leg of the triangles: $\frac{310-250}{2} = \frac{60}{2} = 30$ ft. To find sides *AB* and *CD*, we use the **Pythagorean theorem**: $AB^2 = 30^2 + 40^2 = 900 + 1600 = 2500$, so $AB = CD = \sqrt{2500} = 50$ ft. We can then add each side to find the perimeter of the building: $50 + 310 + 50 + 250 = 660$ ft.

38. The correct answer is 54: In order to find the area of Δ*DEF*, we need to know the values of the base and the height of the triangle. Since Δ*ABC*≅ Δ*DEF*, then *DE* = *AB*, which means that *DE* = 15. Also, since Δ*ABC*≅ Δ*DEF*, then *DF* = *AC*. Therefore, 5*x* – 1 = 3*x* + 3. After subtracting 3*x* from both sides and adding 1 to both sides, the equation becomes 2*x* = 4. Divide both sides by 2 to get *x* = 2. After substituting for *x*, the value of *DF* becomes 5(2) – 1 = 9. Now we can solve for the height, *EF*, by using the **Pythagorean theorem**: $9^2 + EF^2 = 15^2$, or $EF = \sqrt{15^2 - 9^2} = \sqrt{225 - 81} = \sqrt{144} = 12$. Now that we have the base and the height, we can find the area: $\frac{1}{2}(9)(12) = 54$.

39. The correct answer is 37: Dilation changes the length of the legs of a triangle, but not the angles, as proportions remain the same. First note that the triangles are not oriented the same direction but are facing opposite directions, so be careful to match up corresponding angles: angle *M* is equal to angle *Q*. We can solve for angle *M* by adding angles *N* and *P* and subtracting from 180°: $180 - (77 + 66) = 180 - 143 = 37°$.

40. The correct answer is 39: The tree, the ground, and the child's line of sight form a right triangle:

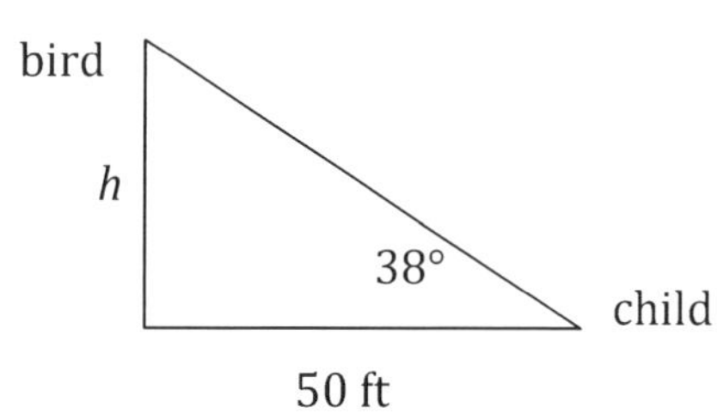

We have an angle and the length of the leg adjacent to that angle. In order to solve for the height of the bird h, which is the side opposite to the angle, it needs to be set up as $\tan 38° = \frac{opposite\ leg}{adjacent\ leg}$ or $\tan 38° = \frac{h}{50}$. We cross-multiply to solve for h: $h = 50 \tan 38° \approx 39.06$ ft. This rounds to 39 feet.

41. The correct answer is 9: We are given two angles and one side. To find another side, we can use the Law of Sines, but we need to know the angle opposite the side we are seeking. So first we must find angle L by adding the other two angles and subtracting from 180°: $180 - (64 + 88) = 180 - 152 = 28°$. Now we can set up our equation. The Law of Sines is $\frac{\sin A}{a} = \frac{\sin B}{b} = \frac{\sin C}{c}$, but to solve this problem we only need $\frac{\sin A}{a} = \frac{\sin B}{b}$. By substitution, that equation becomes $\frac{\sin 64°}{17} = \frac{\sin 28°}{JK}$. Solving for JK, the equation results in $JK = \frac{17 \sin 28°}{\sin 64°} \approx 8.88$. Rounded to the nearest unit, this is 9.

42. The correct answer is 17: We can use the distance formula to calculate the difference between points B and C, which is the length of BC: $BC = \sqrt{(-2 - 6)^2 + (7 - -8)^2} = \sqrt{(-8)^2 + 15^2} = \sqrt{64 + 225} = \sqrt{289} = 17$.

43. The correct answer is 24: We first plot the points to visualize the trapezoid. We can see that the two parallel sides are horizontal and can use the difference in x-values to find the length. We subtract the x-values for two points that have identical y-values. For example, we can take the points (0, 2) and (3, 2) and subtract 0 from 3 to find that the trapezoid has one side of 3. We take the points (7, –1) and (–4, –1) and subtract –4 from 7 to find that the other parallel side is 11. We can find the height of the trapezoid by finding the difference in the y-values. Each y-value is either 2 or –1, so the difference is 3, meaning that the trapezoid has a height of 3. Since the bottom side is 8 units longer than the top (because 11 – 3 = 8), we can divide the trapezoid into a square and two rectangles as follows:

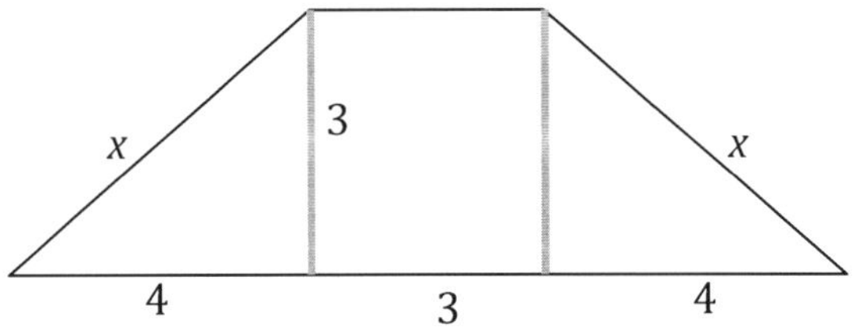

To find the lengths of the diagonal sides, we use the **Pythagorean theorem** on one of the right triangles: $x^2 = 3^2 + 4^2 = 9 + 16 = 25$, so $x = \sqrt{25} = 5$. So, we can add up the four sides of the trapezoid to find the perimeter: $3 + 5 + 11 + 5 = 24$.

44. The correct answer is 76: The central angle of a circle can be found by setting up a proportion: $\frac{arc\ length}{circumference} = \frac{central\ angle}{360°}$. To find the circumference, we must first find the radius or diameter. Since we know the area, we can find the radius: $A = \pi r^2$, so $81\pi = \pi r^2$. We divide both sides by π and take the square root to find that $r = 9$. Then we can find the circumference: $C = 2\pi r = 2\pi(9) = 18\pi$. Then we let θ be the central angle and set up the proportion: $\frac{12}{18\pi} = \frac{\theta}{360}$. Finally, we cross-multiply and divide: $18\pi\theta = 12(360)$, or $\theta = \frac{12(360)}{18\pi} = \frac{240}{\pi} \approx 76.43°$. Rounded to the nearest whole degree, this is 76°.

45. The correct answer is 79: The measure of an inscribed angle is half the measure of the intercepted arc. So $\angle D = \frac{1}{2}ABC$, or $ABC = 2\angle D$. Thus, $10x - 2 = 2(4x + 15)$, or $10x - 2 = 8x + 30$. We subtract $8x$ from both sides and add 2 to each side. Thus, $2x = 32$, so $x = 16$. We can now plug 16 into the equation for $\angle D$: $4(16) + 15 = 79°$.

46. The correct answer is 40: Since $\overline{PQ}$ is tangent to Circle O, $\overline{PQ}$ forms a right angle with radius $\overline{OL}$. ΔOLP is then a right triangle, so the **Pythagorean theorem** can be used to find the measure of $\overline{LP}$. Since the diameter is 30, we know that the radius, or OL, is 15. Therefore, $LP^2 + 15^2 = 25^2$, or $LP = \sqrt{25^2 - 15^2} = \sqrt{625 - 225} = \sqrt{400} = 20$. If LP is 20, LQ is also 20, so $PQ = 20 + 20 = 40$.

47. The correct answer is 21.4: For any point outside a circle, there are exactly two lines tangent to the circle passing through that point. Further, the lengths of these line segments from the point to the circle are equal. In this problem, the two segments extending from *J* both have a length of 10.3. The two segments extending from *K* have a length of 12.6. The two segments extending from *L* have a length of 8.8. The two segments extending from *M* have a length of 7.6. Therefore, the length of side *KL* can be calculated at 12.6 + 8.8 = 21.4.

48. The correct answer is 21: The central angle is $\frac{118}{360}$ of the whole circle, and so the area of the sector is also $\frac{118}{360}$ of the whole circle. We can find the area of the circle: $A = \pi r^2 = \pi(4.5)^2 = 20.25\pi$. Then we multiply by $\frac{118}{360}$ to find the sector's area: $\frac{118}{360} \cdot 20.25\pi = 6.6375\pi \approx 20.84 \text{ in}^2$. Rounded to the nearest inch, this is 21 in^2.

49. The correct answer is 144: We multiply the original surface area by the given factor of $\frac{1}{2}$ twice because surface area is a square measurement (if it was volume, we would have multiplied by $\frac{1}{2}$ three times because volume is a cubic measurement). To visualize this, we can create a simple rectangular prism with sides of 2 cm: $SA = 2lw + 2lh + 2wh = 2(2)(2) + 2(2)(2) + 2(2)(2) = 24$. Cutting each side in half, so that each side is now 1 cm, yields: $SA = 2(1)(1) + 2(1)(1) + 2(1)(1) = 6$. We can see that 6 is equal to 24 multiplied twice by $\frac{1}{2}$. So, using the given surface area from the problem: $576 \cdot \frac{1}{2} \cdot \frac{1}{2} = 144 \text{ cm}^2$.

50. The correct answer is 34: The first step is to calculate how many cubic inches the tank should hold. Since a gallon has 231 cubic inches, and the tank should hold 150 gallons, we multiply: $150\ gal \cdot \frac{231\ cu\ in}{gal} = 34{,}650 \text{ in}^3$. So, this is the volume of the tank. We can use the formula for volume of a cylinder to find the height: $V = \pi r^2 h \Rightarrow 34{,}650 = \pi(18)^2 h$. We divide both sides by $\pi(18)^2$ to isolate h: $h = \frac{34{,}650}{\pi(18)(18)} = 34.06$. Rounding to the nearest inch, the height of the tank should be 34 inches.

How to Overcome Test Anxiety

Just the thought of taking a test is enough to make most people a little nervous. A test is an important event that can have a long-term impact on your future, so it's important to take it seriously and it's natural to feel anxious about performing well. But just because anxiety is normal, that doesn't mean that it's helpful in test taking, or that you should simply accept it as part of your life. Anxiety can have a variety of effects. These effects can be mild, like making you feel slightly nervous, or severe, like blocking your ability to focus or remember even a simple detail.

If you experience test anxiety—whether severe or mild—it's important to know how to beat it. To discover this, first you need to understand what causes test anxiety.

Causes of Test Anxiety

While we often think of anxiety as an uncontrollable emotional state, it can actually be caused by simple, practical things. One of the most common causes of test anxiety is that a person does not feel adequately prepared for their test. This feeling can be the result of many different issues such as poor study habits or lack of organization, but the most common culprit is time management. Starting to study too late, failing to organize your study time to cover all of the material, or being distracted while you study will mean that you're not well prepared for the test. This may lead to cramming the night before, which will cause you to be physically and mentally exhausted for the test. Poor time management also contributes to feelings of stress, fear, and hopelessness as you realize you are not well prepared but don't know what to do about it.

Other times, test anxiety is not related to your preparation for the test but comes from unresolved fear. This may be a past failure on a test, or poor performance on tests in general. It may come from comparing yourself to others who seem to be performing better or from the stress of living up to expectations. Anxiety may be driven by fears of the future—how failure on this test would affect your educational and career goals. These fears are often completely irrational, but they can still negatively impact your test performance.

Elements of Test Anxiety

As mentioned earlier, test anxiety is considered to be an emotional state, but it has physical and mental components as well. Sometimes you may not even realize that you are suffering from test anxiety until you notice the physical symptoms. These can include trembling hands, rapid heartbeat, sweating, nausea, and tense muscles. Extreme anxiety may lead to fainting or vomiting. Obviously, any of these symptoms can have a negative impact on testing. It is important to recognize them as soon as they begin to occur so that you can address the problem before it damages your performance.

The mental components of test anxiety include trouble focusing and inability to remember learned information. During a test, your mind is on high alert, which can help you recall information and stay focused for an extended period of time. However, anxiety interferes with your mind's natural processes, causing you to blank out, even on the questions you know well. The strain of testing during anxiety makes it difficult to stay focused, especially on a test that may take several hours. Extreme anxiety can take a huge mental toll, making it difficult not only to recall test information but even to understand the test questions or pull your thoughts together.

Effects of Test Anxiety

Test anxiety is like a disease—if left untreated, it will get progressively worse. Anxiety leads to poor performance, and this reinforces the feelings of fear and failure, which in turn lead to poor performances on subsequent tests. It can grow from a mild nervousness to a crippling condition. If allowed to progress, test anxiety can have a big impact on your schooling, and consequently on your future.

Test anxiety can spread to other parts of your life. Anxiety on tests can become anxiety in any stressful situation, and blanking on a test can turn into panicking in a job situation. But fortunately, you don't have to let anxiety rule your testing and determine your grades. There are a number of relatively simple steps you can take to move past anxiety and function normally on a test and in the rest of life.

Physical Steps for Beating Test Anxiety

While test anxiety is a serious problem, the good news is that it can be overcome. It doesn't have to control your ability to think and remember information. While it may take time, you can begin taking steps today to beat anxiety.

Just as your first hint that you may be struggling with anxiety comes from the physical symptoms, the first step to treating it is also physical. Rest is crucial for having a clear, strong mind. If you are tired, it is much easier to give in to anxiety. But if you establish good sleep habits, your body and mind will be ready to perform optimally, without the strain of exhaustion. Additionally, sleeping well helps you to retain information better, so you're more likely to recall the answers when you see the test questions.

Getting good sleep means more than going to bed on time. It's important to allow your brain time to relax. Take study breaks from time to time so it doesn't get overworked, and don't study right before bed. Take time to rest your mind before trying to rest your body, or you may find it difficult to fall asleep.

Along with sleep, other aspects of physical health are important in preparing for a test. Good nutrition is vital for good brain function. Sugary foods and drinks may give a burst of energy but this burst is followed by a crash, both physically and emotionally. Instead, fuel your body with protein and vitamin-rich foods.

Also, drink plenty of water. Dehydration can lead to headaches and exhaustion, especially if your brain is already under stress from the rigors of the test. Particularly if your test is a long one, drink water during the breaks. And if possible, take an energy-boosting snack to eat between sections.

Along with sleep and diet, a third important part of physical health is exercise. Maintaining a steady workout schedule is helpful, but even taking 5-minute study breaks to walk can help get your blood pumping faster and clear your head. Exercise also releases endorphins, which contribute to a positive feeling and can help combat test anxiety.

When you nurture your physical health, you are also contributing to your mental health. If your body is healthy, your mind is much more likely to be healthy as well. So take time to rest, nourish your body with healthy food and water, and get moving as much as possible. Taking these physical steps will make you stronger and more able to take the mental steps necessary to overcome test anxiety.

Mental Steps for Beating Test Anxiety

Working on the mental side of test anxiety can be more challenging, but as with the physical side, there are clear steps you can take to overcome it. As mentioned earlier, test anxiety often stems from lack of preparation, so the obvious solution is to prepare for the test. Effective studying may be the most important weapon you have for beating test anxiety, but you can and should employ several other mental tools to combat fear.

First, boost your confidence by reminding yourself of past success—tests or projects that you aced. If you're putting as much effort into preparing for this test as you did for those, there's no reason you should expect to fail here. Work hard to prepare; then trust your preparation.

Second, surround yourself with encouraging people. It can be helpful to find a study group, but be sure that the people you're around will encourage a positive attitude. If you spend time with others who are anxious or cynical, this will only contribute to your own anxiety. Look for others who are motivated to study hard from a desire to succeed, not from a fear of failure.

Third, reward yourself. A test is physically and mentally tiring, even without anxiety, and it can be helpful to have something to look forward to. Plan an activity following the test, regardless of the outcome, such as going to a movie or getting ice cream.

When you are taking the test, if you find yourself beginning to feel anxious, remind yourself that you know the material. Visualize successfully completing the test. Then take a few deep, relaxing breaths and return to it. Work through the questions carefully but with confidence, knowing that you are capable of succeeding.

Developing a healthy mental approach to test taking will also aid in other areas of life. Test anxiety affects more than just the actual test—it can be damaging to your mental health and even contribute to depression. It's important to beat test anxiety before it becomes a problem for more than testing.

Study Strategy

Being prepared for the test is necessary to combat anxiety, but what does being prepared look like? You may study for hours on end and still not feel prepared. What you need is a strategy for test prep. The next few pages outline our recommended steps to help you plan out and conquer the challenge of preparation.

Step 1: Scope Out the Test

Learn everything you can about the format (multiple choice, essay, etc.) and what will be on the test. Gather any study materials, course outlines, or sample exams that may be available. Not only will this help you to prepare, but knowing what to expect can help to alleviate test anxiety.

Step 2: Map Out the Material

Look through the textbook or study guide and make note of how many chapters or sections it has. Then divide these over the time you have. For example, if a book has 15 chapters and you have five days to study, you need to cover three chapters each day. Even better, if you have the time, leave an extra day at the end for overall review after you have gone through the material in depth.

If time is limited, you may need to prioritize the material. Look through it and make note of which sections you think you already have a good grasp on, and which need review. While you are studying, skim quickly through the familiar sections and take more time on the challenging parts.

Write out your plan so you don't get lost as you go. Having a written plan also helps you feel more in control of the study, so anxiety is less likely to arise from feeling overwhelmed at the amount to cover.

Step 3: Gather Your Tools

Decide what study method works best for you. Do you prefer to highlight in the book as you study and then go back over the highlighted portions? Or do you type out notes of the important information? Or is it helpful to make flashcards that you can carry with you? Assemble the pens, index cards, highlighters, post-it notes, and any other materials you may need so you won't be distracted by getting up to find things while you study.

If you're having a hard time retaining the information or organizing your notes, experiment with different methods. For example, try color-coding by subject with colored pens, highlighters, or post-it notes. If you learn better by hearing, try recording yourself reading your notes so you can listen while in the car, working out, or simply sitting at your desk. Ask a friend to quiz you from your flashcards, or try teaching someone the material to solidify it in your mind.

Step 4: Create Your Environment

It's important to avoid distractions while you study. This includes both the obvious distractions like visitors and the subtle distractions like an uncomfortable chair (or a too-comfortable couch that makes you want to fall asleep). Set up the best study environment possible: good lighting and a comfortable work area. If background music helps you focus, you may want to turn it on, but otherwise keep the room quiet. If you are using a computer to take notes, be sure you don't have any other windows open, especially applications like social media, games, or anything else that could distract you. Silence your phone and turn off notifications. Be sure to keep water close by so you stay hydrated while you study (but avoid unhealthy drinks and snacks).

Also, take into account the best time of day to study. Are you freshest first thing in the morning? Try to set aside some time then to work through the material. Is your mind clearer in the afternoon or evening? Schedule your study session then. Another method is to study at the same time of day that you will take the test, so that your brain gets used to working on the material at that time and will be ready to focus at test time.

Step 5: Study!

Once you have done all the study preparation, it's time to settle into the actual studying. Sit down, take a few moments to settle your mind so you can focus, and begin to follow your study plan. Don't give in to distractions or let yourself procrastinate. This is your time to prepare so you'll be ready to fearlessly approach the test. Make the most of the time and stay focused.

Of course, you don't want to burn out. If you study too long you may find that you're not retaining the information very well. Take regular study breaks. For example, taking five minutes out of every hour to walk briskly, breathing deeply and swinging your arms, can help your mind stay fresh.

As you get to the end of each chapter or section, it's a good idea to do a quick review. Remind yourself of what you learned and work on any difficult parts. When you feel that you've mastered the material, move on to the next part. At the end of your study session, briefly skim through your notes again.

But while review is helpful, cramming last minute is NOT. If at all possible, work ahead so that you won't need to fit all your study into the last day. Cramming overloads your brain with more information than it can process and retain, and your tired mind may struggle to recall even previously learned information when it is overwhelmed with last-minute study. Also, the urgent nature of cramming and the stress placed on your brain contribute to anxiety. You'll be more likely to go to the test feeling unprepared and having trouble thinking clearly.

So don't cram, and don't stay up late before the test, even just to review your notes at a leisurely pace. Your brain needs rest more than it needs to go over the information again. In fact, plan to finish your studies by noon or early afternoon the day before the test. Give your brain the rest of the day to relax or focus on other things, and get a good night's sleep. Then you will be fresh for the test and better able to recall what you've studied.

Step 6: Take a Practice Test

Many courses offer sample tests, either online or in the study materials. This is an excellent resource to check whether you have mastered the material, as well as to prepare for the test format and environment.

Check the test format ahead of time: the number of questions, the type (multiple choice, free response, etc.), and the time limit. Then create a plan for working through them. For example, if you have 30 minutes to take a 60-question test, your limit is 30 seconds per question. Spend less time on the questions you know well so that you can take more time on the difficult ones.

If you have time to take several practice tests, take the first one open book, with no time limit. Work through the questions at your own pace and make sure you fully understand them. Gradually work up to taking a test under test conditions: sit at a desk with all study materials put away and set a timer. Pace yourself to make sure you finish the test with time to spare and go back to check your answers if you have time.

After each test, check your answers. On the questions you missed, be sure you understand why you missed them. Did you misread the question (tests can use tricky wording)? Did you forget the information? Or was it something you hadn't learned? Go back and study any shaky areas that the practice tests reveal.

Taking these tests not only helps with your grade, but also aids in combating test anxiety. If you're already used to the test conditions, you're less likely to worry about it, and working through tests until you're scoring well gives you a confidence boost. Go through the practice tests until you feel comfortable, and then you can go into the test knowing that you're ready for it.

Test Tips

On test day, you should be confident, knowing that you've prepared well and are ready to answer the questions. But aside from preparation, there are several test day strategies you can employ to maximize your performance.

First, as stated before, get a good night's sleep the night before the test (and for several nights before that, if possible). Go into the test with a fresh, alert mind rather than staying up late to study.

Try not to change too much about your normal routine on the day of the test. It's important to eat a nutritious breakfast, but if you normally don't eat breakfast at all, consider eating just a protein bar. If you're a coffee drinker, go ahead and have your normal coffee. Just make sure you time it so that the caffeine doesn't wear off right in the middle of your test. Avoid sugary beverages, and drink enough water to stay hydrated but not so much that you need a restroom break 10 minutes into the test. If your test isn't first thing in the morning, consider going for a walk or doing a light workout before the test to get your blood flowing.

Allow yourself enough time to get ready, and leave for the test with plenty of time to spare so you won't have the anxiety of scrambling to arrive in time. Another reason to be early is to select a good seat. It's helpful to sit away from doors and windows, which can be distracting. Find a good seat, get out your supplies, and settle your mind before the test begins.

When the test begins, start by going over the instructions carefully, even if you already know what to expect. Make sure you avoid any careless mistakes by following the directions.

Then begin working through the questions, pacing yourself as you've practiced. If you're not sure on an answer, don't spend too much time on it, and don't let it shake your confidence. Either skip it and come back later, or eliminate as many wrong answers as possible and guess among the remaining ones. Don't dwell on these questions as you continue—put them out of your mind and focus on what lies ahead.

Be sure to read all of the answer choices, even if you're sure the first one is the right answer. Sometimes you'll find a better one if you keep reading. But don't second-guess yourself if you do immediately know the answer. Your gut instinct is usually right. Don't let test anxiety rob you of the information you know.

If you have time at the end of the test (and if the test format allows), go back and review your answers. Be cautious about changing any, since your first instinct tends to be correct, but make sure you didn't misread any of the questions or accidentally mark the wrong answer choice. Look over any you skipped and make an educated guess.

At the end, leave the test feeling confident. You've done your best, so don't waste time worrying about your performance or wishing you could change anything. Instead, celebrate the successful completion of this test. And finally, use this test to learn how to deal with anxiety even better next time.

Review Video: Test Anxiety
Visit mometrix.com/academy and enter code: 100340

Important Qualification

Not all anxiety is created equal. If your test anxiety is causing major issues in your life beyond the classroom or testing center, or if you are experiencing troubling physical symptoms related to your anxiety, it may be a sign of a serious physiological or psychological condition. If this sounds like your situation, we strongly encourage you to seek professional help.

Online Resources

Due to our efforts to try to keep this book to a manageable length, we've created a link that will give you access to all of your online resources:

mometrix.com/resources719/ssreggeometry

It's Your Moment, Let's Celebrate It!

Share your story @mometrixtestpreparation